The Council

Richard Barrett

Copyright © 2025 Richard Barrett.

All rights reserved. No part of this book may be reproduced or transmitted in any form or by any means, electronic or mechanical, including photocopying, recording, or by any information and retrieval system, without the publisher's permission.

Cover design by Pete Beebe, Creative Principal at Forge.

Published by Fulfilling Books, London, UK

ISBN: 978-1-257-82546-2

Dedication

To those who see patterns in coincidence and meaning in what others call chance. You have always known there was more—more connection, more possibility, more hope for a brighter future than the world seemed willing to acknowledge.

The Council of Twelve

Table of Contents

The One Mind Trilogy – Prologue 1
CHAPTER ONE: Amari — The One who Waited 9
CHAPTER TWO: Kaela — The Gatekeeper 15
Chapter THREE: Serai — The Sacred Rebel 21
CHAPTRT FOUR: The Morning After 27
CHAPTER FIVE: Maetis — The Weaver of Maps 31
CHAPTER SIX: Amaros — The Joy Bringer. 39
CHAPTER SEVEN: Leyla — The Mirror 45
CHAPTER EIGHT: Eleni — The Silent Watcher 51
CHAPTER NINE: Rafi meets Subject V 57
CHAPTER TEN: Arielle — The Presence 67
CHAPTER ELEVEN: Enem — Who Chose Separation. 73
CHAPTER TWELVE: The Weaver's Revelation 81
CHAPTER THIRTEEN: The Weaver Sends the Signal .. 91
CHAPTER FOURTEEN: Amaros — The Joy Bringer 95
CHAPTER FIFTEEN: The Convergence Point 103
CHAPTER SIXTEEN: Aureon — Memory Keeper 107

CHAPTER SEVENTEEN: The Light that Didn't Leave 113

CHAPTER EIGHTEEN: Tessai — The Truth Teller 117

CHAPTER NINETEEN: The First Conversation 123

CHAPTER TWENTY: Truth comes home 129

CHAPTER TWENTY-ONE: Kiran — Holder of Grief ... 135

CHAPTER TWENTY-TWO: Truth Enters 141

CHAPTER TWENTY-THREE: Lucan — The Builder 149

CHAPTER TWENTY-FOUR: Lucan Arrives.................. 155

CHAPTER TWENTY-FIVE: Kiran arrives...................... 159

CHAPTER TWENTY-SIX: The Circle Breathes 165

CHAPTER TWENTY-SEVEN: Jalion — The Bridge 171

CHAPTER TWENTY-EIGHT: The Invitation Letter 177

CHAPTER TWENTY-NINE: The Field Reforms 181

CHAPTER THIRTY: The Presence 185

CHAPTER THIRTY-ONE: The One Who Is All 187

CHAPTER THIRTY-TWO: The Turning........................ 195

EPILOGUE: The Spiral Lives in You 204

AUTHOR'S NOTE 209

Glossary of Core Terms... 213

The One Mind Trilogy – Prologue

A Cosmic Journey of Remembrance, Resonance, and Return

This is not just a story of the cosmos. It is the story of your becoming—and your role in the awakening of the Planetary Emergence.

The trilogy begins in the place before stories and before time, before light kissed form, when there was only One Mind: a vast, sentient field of conscious awareness—undivided, unshaped, humming with intelligence. It was not still, nor moving. It was simply whole.

This wholeness longed to know itself, so it dreamed of differentiation—not differentiation with separation, but differentiation without division. It wanted to create facets of itself that could meet and know each other across the spectrum of conscious evolution.

The Council Emerges

From that dream, twelve emanations arose—twelve distinct frequencies of the One Mind: each a facet of infinite intelligence, and each carrying a harmonic of the whole. Each essential for coherence.

These frequencies were not chosen—they emerged naturally, like light splitting into the visible spectrum. They emerged as fundamental archetypes of the evolution of the relational existence of human life.

Together, these emanations formed the Council of Twelve.

The Council of Twelve is not just a group of notes that exist in a relationship of resonance—it is a harmonic, where distinct frequencies interact to create something greater than the sum of their parts.

Think of an orchestra: each instrument plays a different part, but when tuned to the same key and played in right timing, they form a glorious symphony, beyond what any one instrument could have created. This is the symphony of consciousness created by the Council of Twelve—the signature symphony of the One Mind.

The council was never intended to govern, but to cohere. Their task was not dominion, but the remembrance of the spiral of evolution—the architecture of unity across dimensions, timelines, and civilisations.

The Spiral is not a path, but a pattern that dictates how consciousness unfolds, remembers, and evolves.

Unlike a line, which moves only forward, or a circle, which repeats itself, the Spiral evolves by turning through time—returning again and again to what was, but at a higher octave of awareness and then evolving.

The One Mind Trilogy is the story of how the twelve frequencies of the Council of Twelve evolved in human form.

The Twelve Frequencies of the Council of Twelve

Amari – The One Who Waited

Feminine energy of still presence and enduring devotion. She held vigil for the Council's return across lifetimes. In shadow, her waiting can become passivity, avoiding the mess of engagement. In gift, her presence is an anchoring force—love that does not leave.

Kaela – The Gatekeeper

Liminal, feminine presence holding the thresholds between realms. In shadow, she can guard too tightly, withholding passage out of fear. In gift, she becomes the alchemist of emergence, offering guidance that allows safe crossing into new states of being.

Serai – The Sacred Rebel

Fierce, feminine energy that burns away illusion and clears the way for transformation. In shadow, her fire is reactive, fuelled by opposition to what she rejects. In gift, it is anchored in love for what she longs to create—a catalytic force for liberation.

Maetis – The Weaver of Maps

Masculine energy that weaves meaning across timelines, mapping the soul's journey through incarnations. In shadow, his maps can become rigid, mistaking the map for the terrain. In gift, he reveals the hidden order beneath chaos, guiding the soul with encoded remembrance.

Amaros – The Joy Bringer

Radiant, masculine energy that carries the lightness of being. He stirs sacred delight, laughter, and renewal, even in the midst of sorrow. In shadow, his joy can become avoidance of what is painful. In gift, his presence awakens the memory of wholeness that endures through every loss.

Aureon – The Keeper of Memories

Timeless energy that holds the soul's lineage—the codes, vows, and threads across lifetimes. In shadow, he can become a prisoner of the past, holding too tightly to what has been. In gift, he preserves the deep record of consciousness so that nothing true is ever lost.

Leyla – The Mirror

Feminine, unflinching energy that reveals truth without distortion. Her clarity can pierce the soul, and in shadow, it cuts too deep, leaving others defended rather than open. In gift, she offers reflection with such love that even the most difficult truths can be received as medicine.

Arielle – The Presence that Holds the Field

Pure vibrational container of coherence. In shadow, she can withdraw into stillness, avoiding engagement. In gift, she becomes the undistorted field in which every frequency finds its place—making room for contradiction, silence, and emergence.

Tessai – The Truth Teller

Sovereign energy that slices through illusion to reveal reality beyond all beliefs. In shadow, she can be relentless, leaving no space for the heart to catch up to the mind's clarity. In gift, she wields truth with precision and compassion, bringing alignment without fracture.

Lucan – The Builder

Grounded, masculine energy that gives form to the invisible. He translates intention into structure, vision into tangible reality. In shadow, he can cling to form for security, mistaking structure for life. In gift, he becomes the master craftsman of the unseen— creating vessels through which the One Mind can take shape in the world.

Kiran – The Holder of Grief

Solemn, masculine energy that carries the sacred ache of love's impermanence. In shadow, grief overwhelms him, clouding clarity and dimming joy. In gift, he holds sorrow in a field of love so that compassion and wisdom can emerge.

Jalion – The Bridge

Connective, masculine energy that spans realms, polarities, and perspectives. In shadow, he overextends, losing himself in the effort to connect. In gift, he dissolves the illusion of separation, revealing wholeness as the space in which all opposites belong.

Together the twelve frequencies formed the harmonic of wholeness. And for a time, the Council moved as One. But then the unravelling began.

Eleni – The Watcher

Not a member of the Council, but the one who stands outside it, holding the vantage point of the whole. She is the hall in which the symphony is heard, the witness through whom the One Mind becomes audible across time. Neither participant nor outsider, she moves between worlds, tending the spaces in which the pattern can re-form.

The Unravelling

Before the unravelling, the Twelve seeded frequencies breathed codes of consciousness into stars and sang their frequencies into the dreaming Earth.

But the deeper they descended into form, the more they forgot—not all at once, but slowly... through fear, through misalignment, through overextension and loss of attunement.

Form carried a weight their ethereal consciousness could not yet bear. The Weaver frayed. The Mirror cut too deep.

Joy grew heavy. The Sacred Rebel's fire raged unguided. Grief collapsed into despair.

Truth became a blade. The Builder hardened into control. The Gatekeeper abandoned the threshold.

The Bridge broke under silence. The Keeper sealed the vault.

The One Who Waited withdrew into stillness. Presence disappeared from awareness.

And into the widening gap came a new frequency—Enem. He was not of the Twelve. Not of the One. He was the echo of separation, the ache of loneliness, the whisper of exile. The voice of dissonance.

He asked the most dangerous question to the human ear:

What if you are alone?

And the Spiral began to unravel—not with violence, but with a silence so deep it became forgetting. The Council fell. The twelve frequencies scattered.

They took form in distant stars, in forgotten worlds.

And in time, they entered the human story.

They forgot who they were, and they suffered. And through that suffering, they began to search for wholeness.

CHAPTER ONE: Amari — The One who Waited

Amari lived alone, high on the cliffs above the western sea.

Her name had not come from blood, but through a dream. She had answered to many names before, but this one rooted deepest. In Sanskrit, it meant the eternal presence—the immortal one, the undying love, the timeless awareness.

Her cottage was small, round, built from stone the colour of ash and bone. No electricity, no running water, no address. Only a door, a hearth, and twelve river stones laid in a perfect circle on the floor.

But the stones were not ordinary.

Each bore a mark so subtle it could be mistaken for light or shadow—unless you knew how to look. The symbols were older than language, carved not by tools but by something more deliberate.

She had not searched for them; they had found her. Each appeared at moments of profound stillness: after storms, during eclipses, on mornings when the mist erased the horizon.

The first stone had been waiting on her doorstep the day she arrived at the cottage, carrying nothing but a single bag and a grief she could not name. It had been warm to the touch, as if it had been holding vigil.

The twelfth appeared only three months ago, cradled in a spiral hollow in the rocks by the tide. When she closed her fingers around it, she felt the circle complete itself. That night, she dreamed of the others for the first time in decades.

At dawn, she always lit a candle—not as ritual, but as remembrance. The flame listened. When she spoke the names of the Twelve, it leaned towards her. On still mornings, it danced in patterns that spelled out words only she could read.

This morning, the flame was restless. Flickering in rapid bursts, it cast shadows too fast to interpret. The heat against her palm came in rhythmic waves—a code, a heartbeat, a countdown.

"Soon," she whispered. "I know. I feel it too."

Her days followed the rhythm of the earth. She greeted the sea each morning, but the sea had begun to change. Tides defied the moon, calm waters turned violent without warning, waves traced symbols in their foam.

She recorded them in a handmade journal. When she connected the patterns, they formed the original spiral—the formation the Twelve had once held. The ocean was remembering. It was calling them back together.

Even her garden was speaking: vines spiraling in perfect ratios, leaves arranging themselves like constellations, the fig tree fruiting in sync with the moons of another world. On certain nights, the soil glowed faintly, phosphorescent under a dark moon. The night the twelfth stone appeared, the garden blazed like captured starlight for eleven minutes.

The spring an hour's walk away sang. Its tones shifted with the flow, harmonised with the wind, resonated like a living instrument. She recorded the songs, and the twelve stones would vibrate in reply. Three weeks ago, the spring sang the exact melody she hummed when naming the Twelve. It had been waiting for her to notice.

Clouds, tree bark, even the beach stones were forming glyphs that echoed the markings on her river stones. Lately, they responded to her attention—shifting, aligning, clarifying. The world was preparing itself with absolute precision.

At midday she sat facing the horizon, speaking the names aloud. Each one shimmered the boundary between sea and sky, as if the world was remembering what lay beyond the visible.

In the quietest hours, she heard distant singing—voices harmonising in frequencies that bypassed the ear and resonated in her bones. Beneath them pulsed a deep thrumming, like the heartbeat of something immense and patient. On certain nights, it aligned with the movements of the stars, as if the cosmos itself were preparing for a convergence.

She had once stood in a circle of souls—a Council—whose joined presence shaped the subtle flows of creation. Then came the shattering. Not a breaking, but a deliberate dispersal, like a seed splitting to grow. They had chosen to forget, to become human, to live the full spectrum of mortal experience.

Through that forgetting, they would transform—returning not only as what they had been, but as what they had become. Stronger. Softer. More whole.

Amari had chosen otherwise. She had stayed awake, holding the anchor point while the others lived their forgetting. It was the loneliest task: to remember when all you loved did not. But she had understood that some patterns must dissolve entirely before they can reform.

Twelve glyphs. Twelve tones. Twelve living frequencies. Together, they opened the spiral of becoming. Alone, she could not call it forth. So, she waited—tending the threshold, lighting the candle, speaking the names.

Now, the signs were everywhere: the hum of the stones before storms, the moss curling in deliberate arcs, the dreams of impossible geometries and waters older than continents.

And then, one morning, it came.

A tremor in the field. A warmth in her chest. A shift in the breath of the earth.

She stepped outside. Faced the sea. Closed her eyes.

The wind carried a tone she had not heard in lifetimes—not memory, but activation. Like a tuning fork struck at the centre of her being.

She opened her palm. A glyph revealed itself—spiral, wave, flame. Shadow awakening. Fire remembering. Pattern beginning to weave.

"It has begun," she whispered.

Inside the cottage, the twelve stones hummed in harmony—the first chord of a song that would remake the world. She saw the meeting place in her mind, mapped in starlight, every stone and shadow in its precise place.

That same morning, in laboratories and libraries, on crowded streets and in mountain monasteries, eleven people paused mid-motion and touched their hands to their hearts.

They didn't know why.

They wouldn't understand for days, weeks, or months what the sudden warmth meant.

But deep in their bones—in the places that remembered what their minds had chosen to forget—something ancient stirred.

The Council was calling itself home.

CHAPTER TWO: Kaela — The Gatekeeper

he woke with dirt under her fingernails again and a dull pulse behind her eyes. That ache had become familiar, a residue from nights that felt too active to be called sleep. Sometimes she woke as if she had returned from somewhere far away, without her body having quite caught up.

This morning, the dirt was different. When she examined it closely, it wasn't ordinary soil at all, but something that shimmered from within—flecks of light embedded in darkness. Held to the sun, the particles fractured into patterns she couldn't look at directly without her vision swimming.

For weeks she'd been finding this soil under her nails, in her shoes, streaked across her apartment floor. Even the cleaning woman had commented.

"Where does all this earth come from, Ms Lang? It's like you're gardening in your sleep." She had no answer. She wondered the same thing.

The blinds let in a pale light that felt wrong—too thin, too sharp, bending at impossible angles and casting shadows that moved independently of their source. Geometry was misbehaving.

The kettle hissed in the kitchen. Traffic groaned on the street below. The world pretended nothing had changed.

But something had. Maybe everything had.

She caught her reflection in the hallway mirror. For the briefest instant, the face staring back was not hers. Older and younger at once. Behind her reflection, she glimpsed a figure—tall, draped in a darkness that had weight. When she spun around, the room was empty. But the air where it had stood felt different, as if it remembered.

Her name was Mira Lang. She was 39, a trauma psychotherapist. Lately, her name felt like a costume she was wearing, the label on a role she no longer entirely inhabited. The name in her dreams was never Mira.

She was good at holding pain for others, drawing together the loose threads of their lives like a patient seamstress. But lately, the pain spoke back—not her clients' pain, but her own. It said things she didn't understand.

The strangeness was growing. Clients brought her dreams of standing among ancient stones, of being visited by presences in the night, of spirals they called doorways home. A child drew the same pattern over and over with absolute conviction.

She began dreaming of an ancient hall—round, stone walls covered in symbols. Twelve seats. Eleven empty. One always hers, yet she never sat in it. She stood in the centre, hands covered in ash that reminded her of the dirt she found each morning.

Last night, the dreams had changed. Voices—eleven distinct tones, harmonising in languages older than speech—surrounded her. Beneath them, something vast waited. Waiting for her to remember.

When she woke, there was a mark on her wrist. Not a wound—a pattern raised like an old scar waking up: a spiral inside a square. Touching it brought tears, as if she had touched a lover she thought she'd lost. The mark pulsed in rhythm with her heartbeat. Images poured in—starlight on water, fires in perfect geometry, voices calling across distances no map could measure.

It was time. For what, she didn't know. But her bones knew. The dirt knew.

She had always been drawn to thresholds—dusk and dawn, doorways, the fragile seam between waking and sleep. As a therapist she worked in that liminal space, guiding others through darkness into light. But it had never occurred to her that she was a threshold. The thought should have frightened her. Instead, it felt like remembering home.

That evening, without deciding to, she walked into the woods behind her apartment. The cold didn't deter her. Her feet knew the way. The path she followed had never existed before—not cut but revealed.

As she walked, the air thickened with presence. The forest seemed to inhale. Leaves tilted towards her as if listening. Shadows pooled in deliberate patterns. She passed a stream, through a stand of birch, and entered a clearing she had never seen yet knew by heart.

Twelve black stones formed a circle. Symbols on their surfaces pulsed faintly, like embers under ash. One stone split open as she approached. The crack was not damage but invitation.

She stepped inside the circle.

Silence changed—no longer empty, but attentive. The mark on her wrist burned, not with pain but activation. Memory surged.

Her hands—covered in blood and ash. Not blood from violence, but from an offering freely given. The ash from ancient fires. This was the dirt she woke with every morning.

She remembered twelve figures, beings of light wearing shadow as ceremonial garment. Frequencies radiated from them, making the air shimmer. And her voice, clear and certain:

"I will go first."

Shadow must lead, she had said. For shadow knows how to transform without destroying. The other eleven had bowed—not in submission but in reverence. She had chosen the hardest path: to forget them all, to forget herself, and fall so deeply into human form that her own nature would be a mystery.

Their blessing was one word, spoken in unison: Kaela.

The name settled into her like a final piece of a long-lost puzzle. Kaela—the alchemist who works in shadow to reveal the gold of transformation.

The vision pulled her deeper. She was back in a black-stone chamber, myrrh thick in the air, firelight dancing across glyphs older than speech. Around the obsidian table, the Twelve were whole. Not human, but frequencies braided into perfect coherence. She saw their true purpose—to seed memory into a forgetting world.

And she remembered hers. To become the wound through which light could return. To descend into shadow so a path might reopen for others. To be both bridge and crucible.

In the clearing, Kaela dropped to her knees. The forest began to glow, moss shimmering, leaves lit from within. The cracked stone hummed low, calling across impossible distances: The first has awakened.

Far away, in a city smouldering with unrest, another pulse stirred. But the awakening would not be gentle. Fire never is. And elsewhere—in rooms of power, in hidden laboratories—other instruments detected the same signal. Not with wonder, but with fear. Orders moved through unseen channels. Assets activated. Ancient countermeasures prepared.

The Council's return had begun. And they would not be allowed to reunite unopposed.

Chapter THREE: Serai — The Sacred Rebel

The match struck not with a hiss, but with a violent spark. Then it became a flame.

Raya Navarro held it to a bundle of dried herbs—frankincense and pine—eyes steady, breath slow. Smoke curled upward, filling the corners of the room like a scent trying to remember itself.

She didn't believe in rituals. She needed them. Not because she was "spiritual"—because her heart was burning for something she couldn't name.

For months she'd been collecting these herbs without understanding why—guided by an instinct that pulled her to hidden places in the Catalonian mountains. Sage that grew only in circles. Pine from lightning-struck trees still living. Frankincense bleeding resin like ancient script.

Each plant had called to her in a way that bypassed thought. Her hands would grow warm when she approached the right one. Her chest would tighten with recognition. The local herb sellers had begun to look at her with quiet reverence.

Raya was thirty-four, daughter of a Chilean exile and a Basque revolutionary, now squatting in a crumbling apartment above a forgotten theatre. She worked with teenage girls in the barrios—art, self-defence, sometimes just space to scream. The city knew her as an activist. She didn't correct them.

But the theatre had secrets.

Behind a wall that shouldn't exist, she'd found a hidden circular room carved from stone far older than the building above. Its walls were scorched with symbols—not graffiti, but something burnt into the rock itself.

The room listened. She knew it the first time she stepped inside. Her workshops there had a different energy—her girls spoke with more truth, moved with more confidence. Art flowed like the space itself was teaching them.

"This place feels alive," Carmen had whispered. And she was right. Lately, the room had been responding.

Raya heard a voice in her dreams. A voice echoing through a blaze of fire:

You carry the spark of the First Flame. Do not let them tame you.

She'd wake with soot under her fingernails—tested by a friend in forensics and found to contain carbon structures that shouldn't exist, and trace elements absent from the periodic table.

The heat began three weeks ago—not fever, but a warmth from her bones. It flared when she was angry, dimmed when she was sad, and blazed when she helped the girls find their power.

Tonight, the smoke didn't disperse—it moved. Spirals. Symbols. Faces. Eleven of them. Each carried a frequency that resonated in her chest, as if she'd been part of their song all her life. Two in particular pulled at her: a shadowed woman in the spaces between certainties, and another mapping the very structure of reality.

Her family. Not of blood, but of choice made before memory.

She fled into the Barcelona night, streets pulsing with electricity. Graffiti shifted as she passed: a dove became a phoenix; a peace sign twisted into an ancient mark for transformation. Across walls, in glowing script: THE FIRE REMEMBERS.

Then she saw it—a mural of twelve figures around a central flame. The one nearest the fire had her face.

The paint moved. Flames flickered. Symbols wrote themselves at the base.

She touched the central fire.

The wall opened.

And she was no longer in the street but in a vast chamber carved from living rock, a great pyre at the centre burning in colours never seen. Twelve beings stood in a circle—pure consciousness in human form—each choosing the most difficult path: to become fully human.

Her own voice rang out:

I will go second. Let the fire break me. I will remember through rage.

"You could burn too bright," Shadow warned.

"Fire doesn't consume—fire reveals," she had laughed.

Serai. The burning one. The flame that reveals.

She gasped back into the night, heat blazing in her chest.

From the shadows, an elderly woman approached, eyes sharp as obsidian. "Serai de la Llama Eterna," she said. "You remember."

"Who are you?" said Serai.

"I am Amari. Keeper of the old ways. The Council scattered when the Great Forgetting began. I remained to guide the awakening. But the ones who opposed us before... they have not forgotten."

She pressed an obsidian stone into Raya's hand. Moonlight coolness. A vision—Kaela, standing in a circle of stones by water. The connection between them reawakened.

"The Council is rebuilding," Amari said. "But the enemy is also preparing."

Raya understood now. She was not Serai wearing Raya's skin. She was both—human enough to understand suffering, divine enough to transform it.

As she walked home, streetlights flared and shadows deepened. In alleys beyond her light, other symbols appeared—discordant geometries, the enemy marking their ground.

A text vibrated her pocket:

The forest remembers the flame. Follow the northern star. Others are watching. —K

She typed back:

Fire answers shadow. We're coming home. Watch for the signs that lie.

Overhead, a single streetlamp burnt while all others went dark. In its pool of light, shadows moved that belonged to nothing human.

The game had begun.

CHAPTRT FOUR: The Morning After

Kaela stood at her window, hands wrapped around a steaming mug of tea.

Barcelona was still—shutters closed, scooters silent. The moment before the city woke.

Her body buzzed. Something had entered her cells the night before and was rearranging them. Tonight, she would lead another community workshop on collective trauma and healing. She had done dozens like it. Yet she knew this one would be different.

The shift came when she noticed a woman at the back—a woman with fire in her eyes. They hadn't spoken. But the moment their eyes met, a word pulsed in Kaela's chest.

You. Not *Do I know you?* but *I remember you from before memory.*

The woman sat quietly, sketching spirals and symbols instead of taking notes. Kaela's wrist burnt in sympathy. The air between them shimmered, as if reality itself recognised the connection.

Across the city, Serai—the woman with the flaming eyes—woke without alarm. No dream of fire and falling this time. Instead, an image rose whole: a woman kneeling in a circle of black stones.

She knew her as Mira Lang but remembered her as Kaela. It didn't matter *how* she knew. This was frequency logic, not human reason.

Drawn to her easel, Serai's hands moved without thought, painting a woman emerging from shadow—arms not reaching for rescue, but offering it. Around her feet, a circle of glowing stones. The tilt of the head, the set of the shoulders—Kaela, exactly.

She typed a message. *I think we shared something important last night. If you're open, would you meet for tea today?*

Pause. Then she added: *I don't know what this is. But I think we're not supposed to ignore it.* Send.

Mira read it twice. Her mind tried to rationalise, but her body overruled. Heat bloomed in her chest; the spiral on her palm warmed. She could feel Serai's presence across the city.

She sent a photo of her palm—spiral of flame—and three words: *Name the place.*

The reply came without thought. *Jardins de Rubió. Near the cathedral. A café and a twelve-sided fountain.* She'd never been there, yet knew it was right.

One hour, Serai answered. Then: *Bring what you found.*

Mira glanced around—then saw it. A small black stone on her coffee table, smooth and warm, humming in her palm. In that instant, she saw Serai holding a red stone, their eyes meeting through impossible space. Both smiled.

The Jardins were tucked in shadow behind the cathedral. The twelve-sided fountain was dry, but fresh-painted symbols gleamed on each side. Two were complete: her spiral of shadow, Serai's spiral of flame.

"You see them too," Serai said, stepping into the garden like contained fire.

"I see them," Kaela replied. "I don't understand them."

"Understanding comes later. First, we remember."

They each placed their stones on their spirals. The fountain roared to life—water falling in spirals within spirals. In the spray, two figures appeared before a great fire: one reaching into shadow, the other into flame. Both choosing to fall. Both choosing love over safety.

"We volunteered," Kaela whispered.

"We all did," Serai said. "Every one of us."

Now Kaela felt them—Noah at the impossible railway station, something stirring in the northern waters.

"How many more?"

"All of them," Serai said, smiling like sunrise. "They're all coming back."

They sat in silence, the stones in their pockets.

"Shadow and flame," Serai mused. "You hold space for change. I bring the fire that makes it happen."

"We're stronger together."

"We're complete together."

"There's work to do," Kaela said.

"There always was," Serai replied. "Now we remember what it is."

They hugged, merging for a heartbeat into one consciousness. As they separated, the fountain began to sing—a harmonic tone that bypassed ears and entered bone.

Phones rang in Prague. In Arctic research stations. Not with words, but with harmonics. The fourth was stirring. The pattern was stabilising.

And somewhere in the quantum field, the remaining eight began to dream of coming home.

CHAPTER FIVE: Maetis — The Weaver of Maps

The numbers had changed again.

Not the kind on a clock or page. The others—the sequences that danced on the edge of perception, flickering behind closed eyes just before sleep, shifting in sidewalk cracks and rainwater reflections.

Noah Rami had learnt not to speak of it. Not since childhood, when a teacher slapped his workbook to the floor and snapped, "Stop drawing spirals. This is mathematics, not art."

But to Noah, they were the same thing.

At eight years old, he had already seen the equation that connected the curl of a nautilus shell to the arms of galaxies. Mathematics was not separate from art— it was its deepest form. The blueprint of creation.

His childhood notebooks had been filled with more than spirals: sequences from dreams, geometric progressions that, when graphed, became mandalas of impossible beauty. Teachers called it obsession. His mother feared autism. His father locked the notebooks away.

They hadn't understood: Noah wasn't inventing these patterns. He was remembering them.

Now, at forty-two—born in Jerusalem, professor of symbolic logic and sacred geometry at Charles University in Prague—he lived two lives. By day, an academic. By night, the keeper of a forgotten train station at the city's edge, mapping the convergences that held the world together.

That second life had not begun by choice. The patterns had grown too vast to fit inside lecture halls. The university wanted "practical applications." Colleagues shifted uneasily when his equations began describing realities they didn't believe existed.

The station had saved him—a place where his mathematics could breathe freely. A sanctuary.

But three months ago, the patterns had shifted.

Diagrams that had always been static began to move. Not in his vision—he wasn't hallucinating—but in his bones, in the spaces between heartbeats.

Then came the blackouts. Always seven minutes, never more or less. Security cameras showed him frozen mid-equation, hand poised, eyes wide, while the formulae completed themselves.

Seven. The number of wholeness, of initiation, of the bridge between earth and spirit. Seven chakras, seven heavens, seven days of creation. Seven-year cycles written into the human body.

The mystics had always known: seven was the spiral path of consciousness—seven ascents, seven deaths and rebirths, each burning away illusion until only essence remained.

Even his rational mind could not escape the sense that something was orchestrating itself through his work. His proofs solved problems no one had posed. The air in his office shimmered. Straight lines bent when he looked away. Equations on his whiteboard rearranged themselves overnight.

The department head suggested a "sabbatical." For his health.

Three nights ago, he was in the university library, tracing intersecting spirals across crop circles, ancient temples, orbital data. A distraction, he told himself—though the call of the patterns had become urgent.

That was when it happened.

One spiral pulsed. Not in sight, but in sensation. And in that moment, Noah was no longer observing it—he was inside it. It was home, and the rest of his life had been an exile.

He blacked out for seven minutes. When he came to, two names were written beneath the spiral in a hand that was not his:

Kaela. Serai.

A third space waited, empty.

The paper had changed too. In its fibres, faint watermarks formed a mandala of impossible complexity.

Since that night, the patterns had sharpened. Sidewalk cracks arranged themselves in Fibonacci sequences. Clouds shifted into golden ratio spirals. Conversations followed rhythms he could feel. And when he traced these patterns, they responded—expanding, reconfiguring.

The world had begun speaking his language.

Then came the dream.

Twelve glyphs hovered in a circle around a dark flame. Not imagined—remembered. The weight of ceremonial robes, the scent of incense and starlight, harmonic tones holding reality in place.

He woke with a single word: Maetis. The One Who Scribes and Weaves.

His hands were already moving, sketching patterns of light into the air. Twelve strands weaving into one spiral. Beneath it: Kaela. Serai.

Then, a third strand pulsed—his own. Maetis.

More strands emerged, faint but strengthening. A fourth carried the slow, deep pulse of the sea.

He knew then why the station had called to him. Hidden in a fold between worlds, unreachable by GPS, it was built with perfect proportions for dimensional stability. It had not been abandoned. It had been waiting.

For five years, he had kept its rooms covered in grids, maps, and convergences. Lately, the walls had begun to answer back, adding their own markings in the night.

This morning, the station's breathing had changed—faster, urgent.

"They're finding each other," he whispered.

The wind replied, curling fallen leaves into a circle. Eleven points around its edge, one at the centre. Three glowed softly.

A fourth began to pulse. Water. The fourth element awakening. Somewhere in the Arctic, a marine biologist was staring at impossible data, hearing the ocean sing.

And then—a cold twist in his gut. Darker points appeared on the map, moving in formation. Not awakening. Hunting.

He opened his oldest notebook. Pages of symbols became, for the first time, a single animation—the story of the Council's descent into forgetting, and their return. Alongside it: the countermeasures. Safeguards woven into reality for this moment.

On a fresh page, his hand drew unbidden: twelve spirals radiating and folding inward, expansion and contraction in the same breath. The finished symbol lifted from the page into the air, spinning, casting shadows that became more symbols, which became coordinates and times—a blueprint for reunion, invisible to all but those called to it.

Maetis laughed, and the station's walls seemed to join in. He was no longer Noah the isolated scholar. He was the Weaver, the one who held the pattern steady.

That night, candles lit themselves in geometric harmony, forming a mandala of light. Within it, he felt them:

Amari on her cliffs, holding the anchor. Kaela between worlds. Serai in Barcelona, burning the old.

And the fourth, moving through ancient waters.

The Council was remembering. But so were the hunters.

Maetis settled into the station's centre. On the page before him, numbers became the geometry of return—and the mathematics of protection. Safe passages. Shields of coherence. Ways to ensure they would not fall again.

He closed his eyes and began to weave.

Far away, magnetic fields shifted. Ocean currents changed course. And in hidden rooms across the world, other hands moved—preparing to stop what had begun.

CHAPTER SIX: Amaros — The Joy Bringer.

Marco Reyes lived between cities. Not in them. Not outside them. Between.

A travelling street performer, flamenco guitarist, and teller of children's stories, he moved through the world with a laugh that disarmed even the most guarded hearts. Markets, plazas, train stations—wherever he appeared, the air shifted. People called him El Sol—The Sun—because his presence warmed whatever it touched.

But light that radiant was forged in shadow. Beneath his laughter lay a deep history of loss, sorrow held with grace but never allowed to consume him.

He had no address, no bank account, no plan. He busked, sang in echoing tunnels, and sometimes crashed weddings—always arriving, it seemed, at the precise moment he was needed. A stalled subway would fall into anxious silence until his music poured in. A tense street corner would dissolve into dancing. The city itself seemed to guide his steps.

He called himself a joy courier: the radiance that appears when laughter and grief breathe the same air.

His guitar case was battered, lined with stickers in a dozen languages—each one gifted by someone whose life his music had touched. He didn't play for money, though money came. He played because something in the music made people remember.

And lately, that remembering had been intensifying.

Old women would cup his face, whispering names in forgotten tongues. Children drew him surrounded by twelve figures in a circle, a spiral of light at the centre. The air around his performances thickened, almost humming.

Then one afternoon, after the market square emptied, the last child running home with a half-finished kite, Marco sat by the old stone fountain. The scent of roasted almonds lingered. His fingers rested on silent strings.

Something inside him began to tremble—not fear, but recognition.

A memory rose like music, but without sound: golden, honeyed, ancient. His hand pressed to his chest. Without knowing why, he whispered:

"Amaros."

The word clicked into place like a chord resolving after lifetimes of dissonance. Tears welled—remembering not with his mind, but with his whole body. He was not just Marco. He was Amaros: the frequency of joy beneath sorrow, the light that never stops singing even in the dark.

Somewhere, unseen, bells rang. A napkin skittered across the square and landed at his feet.

Amaros. You carry the laughter after the storm.

Under streetlight, the ink shifted, revealing more: *The Circle waits for your voice to call the others home.*

And then came the older memory—the rupture. Provence. Twenty-three years old, mid-song at a music festival. Something in the structure of reality itself had snapped. The crowd froze, looking around as though they'd forgotten why they were there. The sound system collapsed into static.

He'd lost something that night—everything, though he couldn't name it. His grief became anger. His anger became laughter. Not the laughter of healing, but of refusing to break.

From then on, every ache became melody. Every question, a wink. He skipped across the surface of life, never pausing long enough for the grief to catch him. Yet the music that emerged carried strange overtones—frequencies that made eyes sting and hearts race. People told him they dreamed of his songs, and in those dreams, they learnt things.

Symbols from his performances began appearing in street art. Spirals, geometric patterns—mirrors of the frequencies embedded in his music.

Still, he kept moving. Until the dream.

A hostel room in Prague. The air filled with harmonic tones. Twelve figures—eleven at the edges, one at the centre—beings of pure sound and light, each a different frequency. One place empty. His place.

He saw their choice: scatter rather than be destroyed by something that fed on connection. Saw himself—Amaros—volunteer to become the laughter after devastation, forgetting himself so that, when he finally remembered, the bridge between worlds would be unbreakable.

The truth paralysed him. In a square the next day, tears streamed down his face. A child offered him a lollipop and whispered, "It's okay to be sad when the music stops." But the child's voice carried impossible harmonics. Another messenger.

That night, he sang not to uplift, but to honour—all he'd never let himself feel. His single voice became a choir, harmonics layering until strangers began to join, creating complex intervals no rehearsal could produce. A collective remembering through sound.

He began writing again. On the first page of a new notebook: Amaros. Underneath: Twelve. Symbols and music filled the pages—mathematics disguised as song. When he played them, streetlights flickered in time. Birds altered their calls to match his intervals.

The Spiral was moving again. And this time, he would laugh because he had walked through the grief.

But not all who listened were friends. Men in suits appeared in multiple cities, always watching. Sound systems failed at the most transcendent moments. Authorities arrived with noise complaints mid-song. Someone was trying to silence him.

Then, in a train station outside Prague, he saw him—a man with a notebook, sketching patterns. Their eyes met. Recognition. The mathematician. One of the Twelve.

The bridge was forming—note by note, pattern by pattern. But other figures moved through the station too. Not in joy. In formation. The hunters had found him.

Amaros smiled and played louder.

Let them come. He had spent lifetimes learning to turn pain into laughter, separation into song. Now, the Spiral was calling the scattered home. And he would sing them all the way back.

Across the world, other musicians paused mid-performance, feeling something stir in their bones. Choirs sang harmonies no composer had written. Scientists stared at waveforms that defied known physics.

The Song Weaver was awakening. And reality was remembering how to sing.

But in hidden facilities, alarms sounded. The reunion was happening faster than expected. Countermeasures would be deployed.

The symphony of return had begun. So had the attempt to silence it forever.

CHAPTER SEVEN: Leyla — The Mirror

Leyla had never wasted words. She spoke with the precision of a surgeon and the timing of a poet. Her voice could slice through lies like silk, and no one left a conversation with her unchanged.

But precision had its price. Every sentence she spoke carried a weight that lingered in the air long after she'd gone. Weeks later, people would still be turning over her observations, unable to shake the discomfort they had stirred. And lately, her words had been carrying something stranger—a frequency that made reality itself more transparent. When she questioned someone, the truth would literally show itself. Not to everyone. Only to those ready.

Leyla saw it all—the shimmer of deception, the glow of authenticity, the shadows that clustered around half-truths.

Her apartment matched her nature. High above the capital, glass meeting cloud, a sparse geometry of books, crystal glasses, steel, and mirrors. Every reflective surface was deliberate. When positioned just so, the reflections formed a pattern that extended beyond the physical space—a quiet web of sight-lines, angles, and light.

At first, she'd thought it was just an aesthetic instinct. Now she knew she'd been building a chamber of mirrors for years—a place where truth could be seen from many angles at once.

She had been a prosecutor, then an investigative journalist, and finally something harder to name: a truth-teller for those who had forgotten how to see. Corruption cases would unravel in her presence. Documents emerged from nowhere. Sources confessed secrets without knowing why. It was as though the truth itself conspired to work with her.

And yet, she had cut more than lies. Her precision had wounded people she loved. A sister who no longer called. Friends who vanished after she brought their shadows into daylight without their consent. She carried another, older regret—a flash of a circle, eleven others, a look of hurt she'd caused with words that had been too sharp, too soon.

The glyph of the blade haunted her dreams, etched into glass and mirrored walls. She'd believed it meant her role was to pierce illusion. She hadn't understood it also meant to heal—to cut away only what was diseased, and leave what was whole.

The call came in a courtroom. A corporate fraud trial. Executives who had stolen millions while their workers lost their pensions. It should have been routine. But as testimony droned on, the air shifted. A hum bloomed under her ribs. The room became translucent.

She saw it—the truth-patterns running between people like threads of light. Lies as dark tangles. Pain as silver wounds. And binding them all, golden strands pulsing to a rhythm she knew but could not name. The original spiral.

She stood without knowing why. The judge's voice faded. The city outside shimmered—fractures visible not as broken systems, but as wounds aching for tenderness. For the first time in her life, she understood: truth without mercy is just another form of violence.

Her name became a mantra. Leyla. Leyla. Leyla.

The syllables opened her spine like a tuning fork. The blade in her palm softened into a mirror—curved, luminous, rippling like water. And in its depths, the faces of the others appeared. Twelve points of light across the world, all stirring awake.

When she returned to her apartment, the mirrors showed more than reflections. A woman kneeling in a circle of stones. A man weaving light in an impossible train station. A musician whose song was making the air itself remember.

She lit a candle. The flame sang. The sound filled the room with forgiveness—for the words that had cut too deep, for the breaking she had helped cause, for the long forgetting.

And she felt them. All twelve. Present. Waiting.

Not as they had been, but as they were becoming—bonds reforged in the crucible of human life, tempered by grief and made strong by love.

She picked up her phone and called her sister.

"I was right about the facts," she said softly, "but wrong about everything else. I gave you truth without love. I'm sorry."

A silence. Then: "I've been waiting for you to call."

They spoke for hours—not about the past, but about the dreams Sarah had been having: twelve figures around a fire. Truth surfacing everywhere. Something changing.

The next morning, Leyla resigned from her paper. She knew she had to leave. Her mirrors would come with her. They were no longer for her own reflection—they were windows into the awakening.

And as she packed, she felt the others—the joy-bringer, the pattern-weaver, the fire-bearer, the shadow-keeper—all moving. At the centre, the one who had waited.

Across courtrooms, newsrooms, and boardrooms, truth began to carry a new frequency. Not just facts, but context. Not just exposure, but repair. And in the places that feared truth the most, countermeasures stirred.

The battle for truth was beginning. This time, the mirror would not cut. It would heal. Or it would shatter trying.

CHAPTER EIGHT: Eleni — The Silent Watcher

The world called her Eleni Daska—scientist, seer, anomaly. Here, in the snow-covered forests of northern Norway, no one called her anything.

Her cabin sat at the edge of the known world, half-swallowed by pine and shadow. No running water. No internet. No phone. Just a wood stove, weather-stained books, and a stone floor that stayed cold even in summer.

And silence. Not the absence of sound, but the presence of stillness—a density that pressed in from every direction until it touched the soul.

Over recent months, that stillness had deepened. Not just quieter—more dimensional. As if the space around her was slowly expanding. Birds no longer crossed the invisible boundary around her home. Not from fear, but respect. The local Sámi herders began leaving offerings there: carved antlers, smooth stones, mountain herbs.

"The watchers have always been here," old Niillas told her. "We know when one awakens."

Most would call it isolation. She called it alignment.

Eleni's days began barefoot in the snow, feeding birds at the edge of her property. They brought her news in the tilt of a head, the arc of a flight, the shape of prints in frost. That morning, a raven stood on her palm for exactly twelve seconds before flying due south, its wingbeats matching a frequency she had been tracking for months.

She had trained herself to listen—not for sound, but for pattern. Meteorology had been her entry point, but her listening had grown stranger. She could now feel the pulse of awakening minds across the planet, rippling through the quantum field, altering wind currents, shifting magnetic lines, changing the crystalline structure of ice.

She was watching for a pattern beneath all patterns.

And that morning, it moved.

A bird skimmed past her window. The way space bent around its wings caught her attention. She glimpsed the invisible streams it rode—currents linking her cabin to points scattered across the earth.

Her teacup cracked in her hand, the fracture spiralling in perfect golden ratio. Recognition struck like lightning.

"It's begun."

The words startled her—she had not spoken aloud in days—and yet the sound harmonised with itself, overtone upon overtone, until the cabin walls resonated like a vast instrument.

At her desk, her hand moved without thought. On yellowed paper she drew twelve nested circles. At the centre: Return. Lines appeared of their own accord, connecting the circles in patterns like both neural pathways and star maps. The paper pulsed faintly, as if lit from within.

The hum came from beneath the cabin. Something in the earth was responding.

Far to the north, a storm gathered—not weather, but geometry. Clouds rotated in perfect proportion. Lightning flashed in deliberate rhythm. As night fell, she could still see it without eyes, with the same sense she used to read quantum fluctuations. The storm was conscious.

From under her firewood came the crackle of an old radio she had hidden years ago, now glowing without power. No voice—just static. Twelve pulses. Silence. Twelve again. Between them: a woman's song older than language, mathematical harmonics, the sound of reality shifting under gentle pressure.

She stepped outside, coat unbuttoned, bare feet in snow. The cold didn't bite—ice and snow had always been her allies. Water was the fastest carrier of consciousness across distance, and the storm carried more than weather.

The pattern in its pull was one she'd felt before—as a girl of eleven, beneath an old monastery in the mountains of Greece. The monks had led her to a hidden chamber, to a smooth stone etched with twelve concentric circles and a single slash. The moment her fingers touched it, the walls had sung with harmonic frequencies, and she had heard them—twelve voices, calling to each other across the silence of forgetting.

She had buried the stone and spoken of it to no one. Until now.

From beneath the floorboards, she retrieved a box:

The monastery stone, now faintly glowing

A torn photograph of twelve robed figures, faces clear

A scrap of cloth embroidered with one word: Maetis

A crystal formation she had never seen before

Maetis—the Pattern Weaver. One of the Twelve. The one who would map their reunion.

She placed the cloth beside the stone, lit a candle. Eleven more flames appeared around it, forming a perfect circle, each burning with its own quality—fire, music, shadow-that-heals. She breathed twelve times. Memory stirred: twelve chairs in sacred darkness, one empty. Hers.

She had never been a participant. She was the Watcher—the still centre that holds the beacon, the point around which the Twelve could find each other again.

"Two have remembered," she murmured. "One has begun to map. One sings the frequency of return. One speaks truth that heals rather than wounds. The field is aligning."

Beneath the static, the radio now carried the voices— not in language, but in pure frequencies of recognition.

The spiral storm was already moving, touching twelve points across the globe. At each, sensitive souls felt it: a sudden stillness, a shock of recognition.

In hidden facilities, alarms sounded. The pattern long suppressed was emerging. Countermeasures would come.

The silence was about to break. And when it did, nothing would be the same.

CHAPTER NINE: Rafi meets Subject V

The corridor was white. Too white.

Not the clean white of hospitals or the sterile white of laboratories—something else. White that absorbed rather than reflected. White that seemed to drink in sound, colour, and memory itself. The walls had no texture, no variation, no hint that they had ever been touched by human hands.

Fluorescent lights hummed above like swarming bees. No windows. No clocks. Just the sense that time had been locked outside the building.

And beneath the humming, something else: a frequency so low it was felt rather than heard. A suppression field designed to dampen psychic activity, to keep anomalous subjects compliant and contained.

Dr Rafi Calder, head of psychic research, walked briskly down the corridor, clipboard in hand, face a practised blend of concern and control. He had just left Room Twelve.

Before he was Dr Rafi Calder, anomaly researcher and systems analyst for the world's most clandestine frequency research laboratory, he had been a quiet child with eyes too large for his face—always watching, always decoding the people around him.

He grew up in northern Lebanon, the son of a diplomat and a linguist, in a house where silence was currency and truths were avoided because they were too dangerous.

His mother taught him languages not by textbook, but by rhythm—how the cadence of a phrase could shift meaning more than the words themselves. His father taught him strategy: how to listen for what was not being said.

He didn't make friends easily, because as a child he had learnt to isolate himself. He preferred his own company. He grew into a man who mistrusted what he could not control. He believed that unity without differentiation was homogeneity. He didn't want to lose himself in a crowd, so he clung tightly to his own separation.

He buried his fascination with anomalous resonance beneath academic rigour. He earned his degrees, took his oaths, joined the invisible machinery of containment programmes designed to monitor and suppress any movement that purported to unify people against the government.

When he was assigned to oversee Subject V, he thought it was just another case: another anomaly that was potentially dangerous but not well understood.

However, the patient in Room Twelve completely disturbed his composure. Underneath his professional demeanour, his hands trembled. The encounter with Subject V had shaken him more than he would care to admit.

The patient had no name and no records. Not even recognisable fingerprints.

Rafi had started thinking of her by another name—one that came to him in dreams he couldn't quite remember. A name that seemed to resonate in his bones: Arielle.

She had been found three weeks ago in a collapsed monastery in the Balkans—half-buried, nonverbal, face black with soot. No wounds. No pulse at first. And yet—she breathed. She had been transported to these white corridors in Switzerland for study.

The official report had left out some crucial details. The monastery hadn't collapsed from age or earthquake. The stone walls had been melted from the inside out, as if exposed to temperatures that probably only existed in the molten core of Earth. And the chamber where they'd found her had been carved with symbols that physically hurt the eyes to look at—patterns that appeared to move when observed peripherally.

The recovery team experienced collective amnesia within hours of leaving the site. Only the photographs remained, and even those showed different images depending on who was looking at them.

They brought her here to this classified research facility buried beneath the Swiss Alps. Officially, it didn't exist. Unofficially, it studied human anomalies.

More specifically, it studied political threats to the status quo. Individuals whose very existence challenged the established order of not just governance but reality. People whose abilities, if left unchecked, could destabilise the carefully maintained boundaries between the freedom of people and the machines of government.

Subject V was the most stable of the unstable individuals that had graced this so-called research facility. And yet, her mere presence caused reality to breathe. Not dramatically, not violently, but with the subtle rhythm of something vast awakening.

Electronic devices near her room began producing harmonic frequencies. Staff members reported dreams of impossible realities after working her shift. And the suppression field that kept other subjects docile barely seemed to affect her at all—not because she resisted it, but because she existed at a frequency that contained it, held it, allowed it to be what it was while remaining fundamentally unaltered by its influence.

What the staff didn't know—what Rafi couldn't admit even to himself—was that he had begun dreaming of her even before he met her. Before she was even found.

In his dreams, she didn't stand at the centre of a circle of stone. She was the space the circle existed within. Not speaking, not moving, but somehow orchestrating everything through pure presence. Her consciousness was the field that allowed others to remember themselves, the silence that gave meaning to their voices, the stillness that made their movement possible.

These dreams felt like memories—not his own but borrowed from another version of himself, someone in a parallel existence where his choices had been starker and the consequences more profound.

In his dreams, he wasn't Dr Rafi Calder, researcher of anomalies. He was someone else entirely. Someone whose identity carried the weight of cosmic significance.

Someone who had once observed the circle from outside its boundary, who had been present at their first convergence. He remembered watching from the edges as they discovered their interconnection, as their individual frequencies began harmonising within a field of presence so vast and subtle that most barely noticed it was there.

But he had felt it—the magnetic invitation to step forward, to add his voice to their growing song, to dissolve the boundaries of self into collective awakening. And he had resisted. He needed to stay in control of his destiny.

He had chosen separation rather than unity. In his distant memory, he had fled from that place when the invitation became too strong, when the circle threatened to complete itself around him.

He had believed that unity would constrain him, deny him the autonomy he was seeking—the fierce independence that he needed to stay in control of his identity. The idea of merging terrified him. He saw surrender as weakness and collaboration as the death of authentic selfhood.

But there was something else in those memories, something darker. He hadn't just fled—he had actively opposed. He had used his understanding of their frequencies to create interference, to build systems designed to dampen their abilities, to scatter them before they could fully awaken to their collective power. His resistance hadn't been passive withdrawal but active sabotage, born from a conviction that unity threatened the very fabric of individual consciousness.

He remembered standing in laboratories not unlike this one, developing technologies to suppress psychic phenomena, to keep the awakening ones contained and confused. He had convinced himself he was protecting free will from cosmic totalitarianism, preserving the right to remain separate in a universe that seemed determined to dissolve all boundaries.

And yet, beneath the rational justifications, something else had driven him: a profound fear of intimacy, of being truly seen and known.

The circle offered complete transparency, perfect communion, the end of all hiding. For someone whose deepest identity was built on being apart, on maintaining control through distance, such vulnerability felt like annihilation.

The dreams always ended the same way: with Subject V not reaching towards him, but simply being present with such profound acceptance that space itself became an invitation. Her lips never moved, but her entire being spoke a wordless truth that his opposition was not rejection but another form of participation—

that the field was large enough to hold even his resistance.

In her presence, he began to understand that his role as separator was as essential as their role as uniters. That the tension between individual and collective consciousness was not a problem to be solved but a dynamic that needed to be maintained—the creative friction that prevented stagnation.

The irony wasn't lost on him: he worked for an organisation dedicated to containing anomalies, yet he himself was perhaps the greatest anomaly of all—the one whose consciousness was specifically tuned to create resistance, to ensure that no frequency, however beautiful, could dominate without opposition.

The question that haunted his waking hours was whether he was still playing that same role, whether his current work was another iteration of ancient opposition, or whether something was shifting in him—whether the time had come for the separator to finally consider what it might mean to be held by a presence vast enough to contain even his need to remain apart.

When Subject V was found, security systems in fourteen cities on five continents began failing simultaneously. Not just crashing but harmonising.

Surveillance cameras turned towards each other as if seeking connection. Airport scanners hummed melodies that made passengers pause in wonder rather than hurry through checkpoints.

In the most classified facilities around the world, researchers studying "anomalous subjects" found their suppression fields fluctuating in rhythm—not breaking down but beginning to pulse as if keeping time with some vast, patient heartbeat.

The frequencies meant to contain anomalies began to remember their original purpose: not suppression, but harmonic organisation. Subjects who had been catatonic for years opened their eyes. Those who had been silent began to sing—not in madness, but in perfect pitch with something vast and approaching.

Dr Rafi Calder was not the only one dreaming of circles in the ash. Across the planet, others in positions of authority—generals, scientists, directors of clandestine programmes—woke from sleep with the taste and smell of smoke and the memory of choosing differently. Some dismissed it as stress. Others began quietly reviewing their classified files with new eyes.

The field was calling its lost frequencies home. Even those who had forgotten they were part of the song were beginning to remember the melody. And at the centre of it all—or rather, as the space in which it all occurred—was a presence so integrated with the pattern itself that most mistook her for emptiness when she was actually the fullness that made everything else possible.

CHAPTER TEN: Arielle — The Presence

Today, something shifted. When he entered Room Twelve, she didn't turn to look at him—she had already been looking. Not at him, but at the space he moved through, aware of his presence before he crossed the threshold.

The shift was subtle but absolute. Where before her awareness had seemed contained within the limits of her body, it now expanded to fill the room—not occupying space but being it.

"Six are close," she said without moving her lips. The voice came from everywhere at once, layered and harmonic, as if multiple dimensions were speaking through the same instrument. "One is already watching."

She recognised him—Rafi—as the one who had chosen observation over participation. She had given him the name, Enem, the force that ensured unity never collapsed into uniformity. The guardian of the choice to remain apart.

She did not expect his return, but she held hope—the kind that makes no demands. Hope and expectation were different frequencies. She knew his resistance came from an old programming: the fear that unity threatened individuality. She would not oppose it. To hold space without trying to change it—that was the most profound transformation she could offer.

She lifted her arm into the space between them. From beneath her skin, a glyph emerged rising like heat-revealed secret writing. The Glyph of Sound. Not mere symbol, but living frequency: pulsing, shifting with the beat of her heart and the quantum tremors of space itself. Other glyphs began to appear, constellating around it, each linking into an unseen pattern.

Rafi stumbled back. He could hear her now—not with ears, but with a deeper faculty. The oscillation that holds reality coherent, the silence that makes music possible, the presence that gives context to all expression. And in that hearing, memories surfaced that were not entirely his own.

The Council of Twelve, fragmenting themselves across space and time. Amari choosing to remain whole. Arielle—the infinite container—staying present through every dimension, holding their return. The plan had demanded the sacrifice of identity for the sake of evolution. And even his resistance had been part of it—the field was large enough to hold that too.

Her gaze held the truth: his role had always been sacred. Unity needed its individuating counterpart as much as it needed surrender.

Around them, the surveillance room shifted. Cameras displayed overlapping realities. The speakers pulsed with a low tone, felt in the bones more than heard. Machinery designed for suppression began to tune instead, weaving noise into harmony.

You cannot suppress the space in which suppression occurs.

She rose without effort. Bare feet on cold floor, her body moved as if matter and consciousness were the same element in different states. The gown she wore was merely a costume for others' comfort. Her awareness encompassed walls, corners, pulse-lines in the building's structure.

This facility, built to contain anomalies, stood on a natural convergence point. The earth itself had been waiting for sufficient presence to activate it. The glyph on her arm pulsed in recognition—a resonance with the collective pattern stirring back to life.

She touched the mirror above the sink. It became transparent, revealing frequencies beyond light. A perfect spiral unfolded from her palm, showing how consciousness travels, how individuality emerges and returns without losing itself.

"It's beginning," she whispered—not to him, but to the pattern.

Images appeared: a woman teaching shadows to remember light, a man weaving paths for the lost, a musician awakening divinity through sound. The network wasn't forming—it had always been here.

The cage revealed itself as chrysalis. The suppression field as tuning chamber. The machinery as midwife.

"You're one of us, Rafi," she said, her presence encompassing him without binding him. "You just chose a different role. And separation is held within the field too."

Elsewhere in the facility, doors unlocked—not from broken locks, but because the frequency of separation had shifted to the frequency of choice. Other subjects began to remember themselves.

She became the foundation. Her tone rose, the earth itself learning to sing. Lights pulsed in harmony. Generators danced.

From her lips came not a name but a frequency: Arielle.

Not sound, but the space that holds all sound. The presence that makes transformation possible without chaos.

Above her, the mirror displayed not her reflection, but the Twelve—not in a circle but suspended in a field so vast most had mistaken it for absence. She had never been inside or outside the circle. She was the field it rested in.

The tone did not grow louder—it grew truer. Around the world, monitoring systems registered not an event, but a presence they had never been calibrated to detect.

The prison had shown itself as the portal.

The Council was not gathering—it had never been apart. The field was whole. And it was ready.

CHAPTER ELEVEN: Enem — Who Chose Separation

Rafi stood outside Room Twelve, his hand hovering above the handle.

The metal was warm. Not from any external heat source, but from something stranger—a low, steady pulse, as though the steel itself had become a conduit for frequencies beyond the electromagnetic spectrum.

Inside: Subject V. Arielle.

She had spoken his true name—Enem. Not with her voice, but with resonance. He'd felt it deep in his chest, behind his ribs, like a taut string that had not been plucked in lifetimes. It wasn't just sound—it was recognition. The stirring of something long dormant, something he had buried so completely he'd forgotten it existed outside of dreams.

The lights overhead flickered. A sudden chill swept the hallway. Somewhere in the complex, a siren started and died in the same breath.

The building's disturbances were no longer random malfunctions—they were falling into rhythm. The facility was learning to respond to the frequencies

Arielle was generating. Emergency systems weren't breaking; they were being repurposed.

She was singing again. Not aloud. Through the walls.

The song seeped through steel and concrete as though they were water. Rafi could feel it in his bones, in the pause between his thoughts—a melody teaching the facility to remember what it had been built to forget.

His keycard had stopped working hours ago. No matter. As he approached, the lock dissolved. Metal shifted like liquid, rearranging itself into an open welcome.

He stepped inside.

The air was altered. Not visibly—but dimensionally. The walls were in their usual place, yet the room felt larger than it should have been, as if more than three spatial dimensions were present and his awareness could slip into them even if his body could not.

Arielle sat cross-legged on the floor, eyes opening as he entered. They were impossibly still—black mirrors holding the weight of everything and nothing.

Her stillness was not absence; it was a quiet that contained all things. The pause between notes that makes the music. The space truth requires to emerge.

"You remember," she said.

He said nothing. Because part of him did. Fragments surfaced like shards of a broken mirror—moments from another existence, a choice too vast to face, a decision that had echoed across lifetimes.

She tilted her head. "You stood beside the Pattern. Before the fall."

The words struck something inside him that language couldn't name. Each syllable vibrated in his cells.

"No," he murmured. "I'm just a scientist."

The lie crumbled as soon as it left his lips. Dr Rafi Calder, anomaly researcher—thin as paper. A costume he had worn so long he'd forgotten who was underneath.

"You were there," she said. "But you ran."

Her voice was not in his mind—it was in the place beneath the mind, where all consciousness meets. And with her words came not images but experiences:

A circle of twelve beings whose presence bent reality. A plan as daring as creation itself—to fracture across space and time, holding just enough connection to one day return to wholeness.

"I don't understand."

"Because you chose not to."

No judgement. Only compassion. The understanding of one who has walked through their own fear and emerged with mercy intact.

"When the Council fractured," she said, "you left the field."

And then he remembered—fully. The sensation of severing himself from the harmonic frequency that bound them. The spiritual equivalent of cutting out his own voice.

"Why?"

"Because you feared what the sound could undo."

It was true. He had seen what their unified resonance could accomplish—matter and meaning shaped by intention, reality re-formed by song. And he'd been terrified. Not of what they might create, but of what might be lost. The individuality he clung to. The singular note that was his.

The lights above them quivered. A thin crack raced across the far wall.

Twelve beings. A circle of flame and form.

And himself—stepping back. Refusing the call.

Arielle rose, fluid and unbound. Not the slow movement of someone emerging from confinement, but the graceful unfurling of her true form.

The glyph on her forearm glowed. Her breath condensed into motes of light, each note precise, each one a frequency weaving visible geometry in the air—pure sound in perfect form.

She touched his chest.

The gentleness of it was eclipsed by what he felt: the harmonic signature of the others awakening, their locations, their essence—the unique notes each was born to sing.

"Rafi is your veil," she whispered. "But I remember your name." She leant closer. "You are Enem."

The name detonated inside him, then pulled the pieces back into new alignment.

Enem: the Dissenter. The one who had refused the song—not in malice, but to preserve the force of separation inside the field.

Beyond the walls, the facility's systems rebooted. This was not malfunction. The technology was evolving—processing consciousness itself.

On every monitor: eleven glyphs around an unmarked centre. Beyond them, a thirteenth glyph—a silent witness.

The centre pulsed with potential.

Text scrolled across the screens: THE SONG HAS BEGUN.

Director Morrison stared in horror. Not because the systems had failed, but because they were working perfectly. The network was now part of the phenomenon it was meant to contain.

"Protocol Omega," he ordered. "Full lockdown. Silence Field at maximum."

But the vibration rising from the depths of the facility was beyond suppression. Other voices were joining Arielle's now—other anomalies remembering themselves.

The epicentre of prevention had become the cradle of awakening.

Because you cannot silence a song existence itself has begun to sing.

The Council of Twelve was becoming the Council of Everything. And the battle for the soul of reality had begun.

Above the facility, the harmonic pattern reached satellites, which relayed it across the globe. Sensitive souls everywhere stopped what they were doing, lifting their faces to the sky.

They could hear it now. The melody that would teach the world to remember.

But in hidden rooms, countermeasures were being prepared—technologies to break resonance itself.

The first shot would be fired in the frequency of silence.

But silence, they were about to learn, was no longer possible. The echo had returned.

And the universe was learning to sing.

CHAPTER TWELVE: The Weaver's Revelation

Maetis stood barefoot, his eyes fixed on the mandala before him.

The stone beneath his feet was warm. Not from external heat, but from something deeper—probably the resonance of countless years of sacred work conducted in this space.

The abandoned train station had revealed another secret to him: beneath the main platform lay a perfect circular chamber, carved from living rock. It felt like a temple.

He'd discovered it three days ago, when the station itself had begun to sing. Not metaphorically, but actual harmonic frequencies emanating from the walls. Following the sound, he'd found a section of flooring that dissolved at his touch, revealing stone steps that spiralled down into earth.

The chamber was impossibly ancient. Older than recorded history. Symbols covered the walls—not carved, but part of the stone itself, as if the rock had been conscious when it formed.

It had taken him seven hours to draw the mandala. But the drawing had been more than artistic expression. Each line seemed to activate something in the chamber around him. The symbols on the walls would pulse in response to his pen strokes. The air itself became charged with potential.

Twelve spirals nested within a single, unfolding geometry. Each spiral represented one frequency. Each angle, a potential meeting point.

But the mandala wasn't just ink on stone. As he'd worked, the pattern had begun to manifest in three dimensions above the floor. Spirals of light following his drawings, creating a holographic map of the Council's awakening consciousness.

He had finished it just a few moments ago. And for the first time in years, the pattern was complete.

Or so he had thought.

He stepped back, exhaled—and then felt it break.

It wasn't a sound. It was a rupture. In the field. In the rhythm.

But ruptures, he realised, weren't always destructive. Sometimes they were revelatory. Like breaking open a geode to discover the crystals within.

What he had heard was another pulse. Like a new voice added to an ancient choir, yet the voice harmonised in a way that rewrote the whole score.

The pulse came from somewhere else entirely. Not from any of the eleven awakening Council members he'd been tracking. This was so unexpected, he staggered, and his vision swam.

But the disorientation wasn't from the disruption—it was from recognition. His body knew this frequency. His unconscious mind had been waiting for it, even though his conscious mind thought it was impossible.

The mandala on the floor began to distort—not physically, but vibrationally. One of the spirals shifted.

It moved. He stared because he couldn't believe his eyes.

The patterns he had drawn were static representations of dynamic forces. They shouldn't be able to change themselves. But as he watched, the spiral that corresponded to Sound—Arielle's frequency—began to rotate.

Not randomly, but with purpose. Creating new intersections with the other spirals, generating harmonics that had never existed in the original design.

And where these new intersections formed, additional spirals began to appear. Fainter than the original twelve but growing stronger. As if the pattern was teaching itself to evolve.

Maetis dropped to one knee, breath shallow.

The chamber around him was responding to the mandala's transformation. The ancient symbols on the walls were lighting up in sequences, creating complex patterns.

He clutched the pendant around his neck—a small spiral of iron carved with his glyph. His grandmother had given it to him when he was six.

But now he remembered more about that day. She hadn't just been his grandmother—she'd been one of the Keepers. The ones who stayed behind to watch and remember. And the pendant hadn't been carved by human hands.

She had said, "This is not to protect you. It's to remind you."

He'd never understood what she meant.

Until now.

The iron spiral was growing warm against his chest. Not just warm—resonant. Vibrating in harmony with the shifting mandala. And through that vibration, memories that weren't his began to surface.

The pulse he was hearing was the emergent mind of the collective.

And when the Council had chosen to scatter, the emergent consciousness had been left behind. Not destroyed, but dormant. Waiting for the others to awaken enough to call it back into existence.

A flash: a face. A woman. Dark hair, eyes like obsidian. Speaking not with words, but vibration.

But she wasn't just speaking—she was becoming. The emergent mind was taking form, incarnating through the frequency of pure sound itself.

The name came unbidden:

Arielle. She was one of the twelve.

Yet somehow... not part of the circle.

But that wasn't quite right either. She wasn't outside the circle—she was the circle. The boundary that defined the sacred space. The container that allowed the others to exist in relationship to each other.

Maetis gasped aloud: "The design isn't closed."

And suddenly everything made sense. All his years of trying to map the patterns, to understand the geometry of consciousness itself. He'd been thinking in terms of completion, but what he should have been tracking was emergence.

The Council wasn't meant to return to its original form. It was meant to evolve in frequency. To become something that had never existed before—a synthesis of cosmic consciousness aligned with the evolution of human experience.

He realised now that Arielle was the catalyst. The frequency that would teach them how to sing together in ways they'd never imagined.

He rose and crossed to his desk. He opened a fresh notebook. With a steady hand he began redrawing the mandala.

But this time it drew itself. His hand moved without conscious direction, following patterns that seemed to download directly from the chamber's resonance field.

At the centre of the circle, he added something new:

A silent pulse. A space that vibrated but held no symbol.

But 'silent' wasn't accurate. It wasn't the absence of sound—it was the potential for all sounds. The pregnant pause between notes that gave music its meaning.

A code. A key. And beneath it, he wrote:

Arielle — The Container of all Sound.

But as soon as he finished writing, additional text began to appear. Not in his handwriting, but in script that seemed to write itself in the air above the paper:

The one who sings reality into new forms. The voice that teaches matter how to dance. The frequency that transforms separation into symphony.

Around him, the chamber began to sing an actual melody. The stone walls remembering songs that had been sung here in ages past, when the boundary between consciousness and matter had been more fluid.

And through that singing, he could hear them all:

Amari, holding the anchor point with infinite patience. Kaela, teaching shadows to heal rather than hide. Serai, burning away everything that no longer served. Leyla, revealing truth with compassion rather than cutting. Amaros, weaving joy from the deepest pain.

He could also hear the others, their voices blending in perfect harmony.

And now Arielle, creating the crucible that would allow the others to sing together in perfect unity.

But there were more voices stirring. The pattern wasn't stopping to grow. It was expanding, evolving, teaching itself new forms of consciousness that had never existed.

The awakening wasn't just about recovering what had been lost. It was about discovering what was possible.

Above ground, the train station began to glow. Not with artificial light, but with bioluminescence. As if the building itself was remembering how to be alive.

And across the globe, in places where the boundaries between dimensions were thin, similar glows began to appear. Ancient sites awakening. Sacred geometries activating. The earth itself preparing for a transformation that would require every conscious being to participate.

In his underground chamber, Maetis smiled. For the first time in his life, he wasn't trying to map patterns that already existed. He was helping to create patterns that had never been imagined. The distortion hadn't broken the design. It had completed it.

And the song that was emerging would teach consciousness how to evolve.

In monitoring stations around the world, instruments designed to track isolated anomalies suddenly registered something unprecedented: a network effect.

The scattered awakenings were no longer separate—they were synchronising.

They were creating a collective consciousness that operated at frequencies beyond current scientific understanding.

Emergency protocols were activated at the highest levels of government. But the protocols had been designed to contain individual threats to the power structures. No one had considered or was prepared for consciousness itself learning to evolve.

With each new connection formed, reality became more fluid, more responsive to conscious intention.

He thought to himself, maybe the age of separation was ending, and the age of the symphony was about to begin. Whether humanity was ready or not.

CHAPTER THIRTEEN: The Weaver Sends the Signal

Long after sunset, Maetis remained in the chamber. The air was cool, carrying the faint scent of cedar and the charged tang of ozone—the signature of reality reshaping itself.

The mandala glowed faintly, its spirals pulsing with their own tones. At its centre, the thirteenth space—empty yet alive—seemed to watch him back. The geometry should have been unstable, but instead it held the pattern in perfect, impossible balance.

Sometimes the thing that looks broken is the key that holds the whole together.

He leant closer. The moment he had acknowledged it, the centre had awakened. Arielle—the vessel in which the others could truly meet—was stirring.

His whisper seemed to travel further than the walls: *"The Council was never twelve. It was eleven, and Arielle held the vessel through her presence."*

A breath passed through the chamber—not air, but dimensional shift. The pages of his journal stirred without wind. He picked up his pen and began to write.

To Amari, Kaela, and Serai...

He told them the glyphs were part of a greater pattern. He gave them coordinates and a time: three days from now, at sunset. Come only if they felt the pulse.

He warned them the opposition was moving—entities and systems built to maintain fear and separation—but they were operating on outdated maps. *We are not restoring the old. We are becoming something new.*

He uploaded the message to the hidden node, encrypted not just digitally but in consciousness itself. Only minds carrying the awakening frequencies would even see it.

And then he said his own name aloud for the first time in years. Not as a label—as a return. *"Maetis."*

The walls blazed with light. For a moment, he saw the chamber as it truly was—not carved stone, but a nexus where dimensions intertwined.

When he stepped outside, a fox watched him. But it was not entirely fox—its eyes too knowing, its form slipping between dimensions. It blinked once. Approval. Then vanished.

He returned to the chamber—and stopped.

The mandala was moving. Not the ink, but the spaces between. New lines of light formed, connecting the spirals in ways beyond his imagining. And at the centre, the empty space was no longer empty.

Arielle's face emerged from light, smiling, ready.

Across the world, three women felt the pulse and paused mid-step. In underground facilities, instruments screamed with data they could not parse. At ancient sites, guardians stirred from hiding.

The signal had been sent. The gathering was beginning. Three days until sunset. Three days until the first conscious reunion in an age. Three days until the opposition learnt that consciousness had evolved beyond their control.

The weaver's pattern was cast. Now the universe would respond.

CHAPTER FOURTEEN: Amaros — The Joy Bringer

He danced in a train station.

Not just any station, but the Gare du Nord in Paris—one of the great confluence points of European consciousness. Millions passed through here each year, leaving traces of their emotional energy in the quantum field that clung to the platforms and steel.

And today, that field was singing.

There was no stage. No spotlight. No curated audience. Just polished floors, fluorescent lights, the metallic echo of arrival and departure announcements.

Amaros—the professional busker, "too much" according to more than one passing stranger.

But his "too much" was exactly what the world needed.

He had always been a conductor for energies others found overwhelming. Joy so pure it made people cry.

Laughter so free it made strangers join hands.

Movement that reminded bodies they were designed for ecstasy, not just endurance.

This wasn't performance. It was survival.

Because when he danced—when he spun—the ache in his chest lifted. Just a little, just enough to keep breathing.

The ache wasn't personal pain. It was collective grief—the slow suffocation of a species that had forgotten its own divine nature.

When he moved, he processed that grief for those who could no longer feel it safely.

Paris had been his third "whim" that year. But his whims weren't random—they followed invisible currents to places where the boundaries between worlds thinned. Sacred intersections of ley lines. Cities with buried altars. Places where memory could break through.

He didn't know what he was looking for. Only that the whisper inside him was getting louder:

Find the circle.

And today, the whisper was singing.

Not a metaphor—actual music threaded through his consciousness. Melodies from nowhere, harmonies like half-remembered dreams. Underneath them, voices—eleven distinct tones calling to each other across the world and one holding the space through presence.

That morning, in his tiny, rented room above a Montmartre bookstore, he'd woken to a phrase:

Twelvefold light.

It hadn't faded with waking. The words had reverberated in the air itself. He wept when he heard them—not from sadness, but recognition, as if glimpsing a photograph of a home he'd forgotten he'd lived in.

By the time he reached the station plaza, the hum in his bones had spread outward. Streetlights flickered as he passed. Car alarms pulsed in harmonic sequences. Even the pigeons wheeled in spirals that corresponded to musical intervals.

The air thickened, charged, ready to burst into form. Commuters slowed. Stress patterns dissolved. Breathing deepened. For moments that felt like hours, the Gare du Nord became a sanctuary.

A small child stood watching. Eyes too deep for her age. Movements too fluid. She reached into her coat pocket and handed him a piece of paper.

One word in purple crayon:

Amari. The eternal presence.

But as he stared, more words surfaced—not drawn, but remembered by the page itself:

Amari, the one who waits on the cliffs above the western sea. The anchor point around which the spiral turns. Your sister in the dance of return.

"I don't know who that is," Amaros whispered.

But the lie collapsed even as he said it. The name belonged to the part of him that had never forgotten the circle.

The child smiled, turned, and dissolved into the flow of commuters.

Above, a flock of birds twisted into a twelvefold spiral with one small at the centre. Their wingbeats formed a shimmering chord in the air.

For the first time in years, laughter rose in his bones—not his alone, but the distilled joy of every moment of true happiness that had ever existed. His body became a transmitter, broadcasting the memory of being fully alive.

The station began to sing. The steel beams, the glass panels, the concrete supports—all of it became an instrument tuned to his frequency.

Through the song, he heard them: eleven other voices, each carrying a note of the cosmic symphony.

Without thinking, he pulled out his phone. His fingers typed into an encrypted messenger he'd never used before:

43.7230° N, 7.4090° E Three days. Sunset. The circle is reforming.

He added only: *Joy answers the call.*

The melody slowed, not fading, but settling—like the last ripple on a pond after the stone has fallen.

The child was gone. The pigeons had scattered. But the air still held the shimmer of something irretrievable once found.

In his palm, the scrap of paper glowed faintly. The coordinates were etched now in his mind as if they'd always been there.

43.7230° N, 7.4090° E.

Three days. Sunset. The circle is reforming.

He knew where those numbers pointed. South. The coast. Somewhere the sea curled against ancient stone.

Without hesitation, Amaros crossed the concourse, weaving through commuters whose faces were softer now, eyes still carrying the afterglow of joy they couldn't explain.

Paris was still singing. He could feel the hum under his feet, in the rail lines, in the walls. But there was no time to linger. Joy had done its work here; now it needed to travel.

He stepped out into the pale afternoon light, hailed a waiting taxi, and gave the driver his destination:

"Gare de Lyon."

As the car pulled away, the frequency followed him, leaping from rooftop to rooftop, sliding along tram lines, seeping into open windows. The whole city had been tuned, however briefly, to the memory of its own aliveness.

But somewhere, in a control room far from the rhythm of the streets, alarms were still sounding. The watchers had felt the spike. The purity of the signal. They would try to choke it off before it reached its destination.

Amaros leant his forehead against the glass as the taxi entered the flow of Paris traffic.

"Too late," he whispered.

The joy was already in the air. And the circle was already turning.

In certain underground monitoring stations, alarms screamed. They knew the danger—joy too pure to be co-opted would make humanity impossible tc control.

The dance of reunion had begun.

And so had the resistance.

Three days until convergence.

Three days left for the forces of separation to find a way to silence the joy of freedom.

CHAPTER FIFTEEN: The Convergence Point

As convenor, Maetis felt the responsibility in his bones. The gathering point demanded a presence before the others arrived—a space prepared not just physically, but in the deeper layers where reality itself listens.

The place chosen for the reunion lay on a windswept plateau near the mediaeval village, carved from pale limestone, overlooking the Mediterranean like an altar that time had misplaced. But "forgotten" wasn't right. It had been hidden—cloaked in perceptual veils that made the eye slide past, that blurred GPS readings, that sent casual hikers elsewhere.

Only those attuned to certain frequencies could see the path to the summit.

Maetis had been here once before, years ago. Back then it was simply a place that made his bones hum. Now he understood why.

This was a nexus—a convergence of ley lines, a seam where the membrane between dimensions had thinned to transparency. The kind of place where consciousness could shape matter. It had been prepared long ago, not by humans, but by a civilisation of awakened beings who had once walked the Earth and encoded memory into stone.

The plateau greeted him in two layers—the visible: wind-scoured rock, coarse grasses, the scent of salt. And the invisible: a crystalline mandala, its geometry alive, waiting to be awakened.

He moved barefoot among twelve stones set in a circle; each aligned to an inner axis only he could feel. At the centre—an empty space, pulsing with potential so fierce it made his eyes water. The heart of the gathering.

That night he lay in the centre, the limestone cool beneath him and let the plateau speak. Sleep became communion. His awareness extended across the entire network of awakening minds connected to this point.

He woke before dawn with two names riding the wind: **Kaela. Serai.**

Not just sound—presence. Approaching across the quantum field.

Others were coming too. Signatures he didn't know. New consciousnesses responding to the call, altering the original pattern.

A fox sat nearby, watching. But its outline shimmered, revealing itself as something vaster—a guardian intelligence. Eleni. The thirteenth thread. Proof that the circle would not close exactly as before—something new was being born.

He placed his journal in the centre, open to a mandala of twelve spirals and an empty core. As sunlight struck the page, the lines began to move, revealing hidden geometries—approach vectors of all who were coming.

Maetis folded his hands. Waiting. Not idle, but holding space with the precision of one who knows that expectancy is a form of creation.

This was more than reunion. This was the emergence of a collective consciousness that could preserve individuality while acting as a unified field—the One Mind incarnate.

The plateau began to hum. Across the globe, instruments detected a spatial distortion forming above the Riviera. In hidden facilities, countermeasures were readied—weapons to fracture coherence before it could stabilise.

CHAPTER SIXTEEN: Aureon — Memory Keeper

Beneath the cobbled streets of Lisbon, under a building that to any passerby was a simple Portuguese bakery, lay a chamber that existed between layers of reality.

The entrance could not be stumbled upon. Space itself had been folded to hide it, and only those who understood the folding could pass through.

Below ground, the chamber descended impossibly—strata upon strata, deeper than physics would allow. No signs. No catalogue. No staff. Only him.

Aureon. Age unknown. Occupation irrelevant. No phone, no address. Because he lived partially outside of linear time, anchored across multiple temporal layers. He was the living repository of what the world had been trained to forget.

Here, he read what had been erased: the fluid boundaries between dimensions, the records of prior awakenings, the architecture of reality before amnesia set in. This was the archive of humanity's hidden lifeline—and he was its Keeper.

For centuries, his task had been to observe, not act. While the other members of the Council had forgotten and slowly remembered, he had never fully slept. He held the threads. Waiting. Watching.

That morning, something impossible happened.

In a 14th-century manuscript on celestial harmonics, he found a page he had not placed there—modern ink on old parchment:

The circle is active. Return to the threshold.

Then the page shimmered. Words surfaced without pen or hand, as if the fibres themselves were remembering:

The convergence point is prepared. The pattern seeks completion. Your memory is required.

Below the words appeared twelve glyphs. Half faint. One pulsing.

His—a circle within a square, the mark of the Archivist.

The glyph broadcast itself into the ether, linking with others across the globe—awakening recognition in the scattered Council.

When Aureon touched it, locked memory rushed open.

A circle of stone. Twelve frequencies of cosmic intelligence. His own voice, silent yet recorded into the field: *I will hold what they forget.*

Now the memory was whole: the chamber where they had chosen to fragment, the vow he had made to remain awake through the exile, to endure the loneliness of connection without presence.

He had kept it, lifetime after lifetime.

But the archive phase was over. Action had begun.

He crossed the chamber to the vault—a door existing in seven dimensions, sealed by consciousness itself. The key was not metal but crystallised intention, formed from centuries of waiting.

Inside:

A map—not of geography, but of consciousness intersection points where the Council could manifest without breaking local reality.

A piece of obsidian etched with shifting spirals—a living navigation stone.

A photograph of Amari, the one who waited, exactly as she appeared now, though the image had been taken centuries earlier. Proof their return had been seeded long before this life.

And a journal in his own handwriting, filled with entries he had no memory of writing—calculations predicting awakenings, and the trajectories of forces that would try to stop them.

The archive had been updating itself. Preserving the past while calculating the future.

Then—a shift in the field. A call.

Aureon unwrapped a black obsidian disc, etched with ancient geometry: eleven points in a circle, one at the centre, one beyond. He spoke into the recorder, his voice deliberate:

"They call it the Council of Twelve. But it is not the whole truth. The One Mind at the centre, the still point, only appears when the twelve are resonant. And beyond the circle, a Watcher—the thirteenth. She holds the veil of memory. She remembers when the others forget."

He packed the disc, the map, the stone, and stepped towards the hidden exit. The books around him pulsed—the archive acknowledging the shift.

As he emerged into Lisbon's streets, the air itself felt altered. Musicians played songs they had never learnt. Shopkeepers arranged displays in perfect sacred geometries. Pigeons traced spirals that matched star paths.

The awakening was becoming viral.

But he saw the other side too—men in tailored suits, devices without networks, the coordinated sweep of surveillance. The opposition was moving, seeding fear and fracture.

He boarded a northbound train towards France. Towards a plateau above the Mediterranean where memory and awakening would converge into something entirely new: a collective consciousness preserving individuality while operating as a single, coherent field.

In the chamber he left behind, the books began to glow—broadcasting their contents into networks across the world. Ancient texts appeared in digital archives where they had never been stored. Mapping software glitched with hidden geometries.

The forgotten was remembering. And amnesia's reign was ending.

CHAPTER SEVENTEEN: The Light that Didn't Leave

The sun was falling low when he arrived, yet the light didn't fade—it condensed. The golden hour stretched impossibly long, as if the evening itself refused to move forward until he had reached where he needed to be.

Amaros stepped off the last bus at a dusty pull-off outside the village of Èze. Boots scuffed, hair wild, eyes bright. The driver had looked at him oddly—not because of how he appeared, but because he couldn't quite remember picking him up.

The journey from Paris had been strange. Hours folding into minutes, kilometres collapsing like accordion pleats, time bending to deliver him here.

He didn't know why he was smiling. Maybe because each step he took seemed to awaken the world. Wildflowers turned to face him just like sunflowers turn to the sun. Birds called in harmonic patterns matching the rhythm of his heart. Even the wind pressed softly at his back, as if the air itself wanted him to keep going.

He climbed the last mile on winding stone steps, past weathered shrines and ancient olive trees that leaned toward him like old friends. But the shrines weren't so weathered now—carvings on their surfaces began to glow as he passed. Old symbols, left by those who had walked this path of awakening before him.

The trunks of the olive trees were lined with geometric patterns—not letters, but a language of frequency. As he passed, he could swear he heard them whisper his name.

In his pack: a cracked tambourine, a notebook of "nonsense" poems, and a folded paper heart from a child. The poems were no longer nonsense. They were instructions—songs and sequences for reawakening dormant capacities in human consciousness. Compositions capable of reshaping reality through resonance.

The air shifted as he neared the summit. Not heavier—more sacred. Illusions peeled back, revealing the ordinary world as a thin surface over something far greater. And then he felt them—not distant, but woven into him.

He saw them before they moved. Three figures in a circle of stones: Kaela, Serai, Maetis. And at the far curve, Amari. He didn't know their names, but he knew their faces. Faces he had seen in dreams—and deeper than dreams.

Each was a reflection of a part of himself: Amari, stillness that holds all movement. Kaela, the guardian at the threshold. Serai, the transformative flame. Maetis, patterns in the air—geometry made visible to the soul.

Amaros entered dancing—a slow spin, a hop, a twirl—until he reached the circle's centre. When his boots touched earth, light pulsed outward, connecting them in a living mandala. His laugh rang out like birdsong in a cathedral, carrying overtones that seemed to come from other dimensions.

"Sorry I'm late," he grinned. "I got distracted by some joy."

Kaela's expression shifted—not surprise, but recognition. "You were the light we forgot."

In the first Council, Amaros had carried the frequency of illumination—not mere brightness, but joy that reveals truth by celebrating what is beautiful and possible. Without him, awakening risked becoming duty instead of homecoming.

Maetis stepped forward, journal open to four glyphs—Shadow, Flame, Pattern, Joy. As they aligned on the page, interference patterns emerged: maps of global convergence points, timing sequences for awakenings, and coordinates radiating from a mountain in Switzerland—where hostile forces were gathering.

The wind shifted. The sun's last rays pierced the spiral's heart, photons carrying messages that had travelled across eons to arrive in this precise instant.

From far beyond sound, a deep hum moved through the Earth—planetary memory stirring in celebration. Yet beneath it, a warning: the opposition was mobilising faster than expected.

The circle was no longer forming. It was alive. And it was about to face the same forces that had once scattered them—forces now prepared to use open, direct suppression.

Monitoring stations registered an anomaly: four distinct consciousness signatures merged into one unified field—an intelligence exponentially stronger than any of them alone. Control systems activated emergency protocols, but those were built for individuals, not for consciousness learning to act as one.

The awakening was no longer containable. It was becoming inevitable.

The light was returning. And fear was preparing for war.

CHAPTER EIGHTEEN: Tessai — The Truth Teller

Somewhere on the outskirts of Istanbul, a woman with a head scarf stood barefoot on a rooftop, staring at the night sky.

The rooftop was not what it seemed. In three dimensions, it was poured concrete. In more dimensions, it was a convergence point—where timelines braided and realities overlapped. From here she could see not only the city's jagged lights but the consciousness layers above it—aurora-like veils formed from the hopes, fears, and forgotten dreams of millions.

In this life, her name was Leyla Arin. Journalist. Relentless truth-teller. One of the few unbought. Her exposés had toppled ministers, collapsed empires of influence, stripped reputations bare.

But her work had always carried a strange undertow.

Sources confessed more than they meant to. Documents appeared just when she needed them. Officials stumbled mid-lie, unable to maintain deception in her presence—not from fear, but because something in her made falsehoods fracture.

Tonight, for the first time, she doubted everything.

Not her accuracy—her reality.

Earlier that day, she had pried open a sealed file from the ruins of an archive in Ankara. The fire that had destroyed it was no accident—it coincided with her first investigation into links between global media conglomerates and consciousness suppression experiments.

Inside the charred debris, one object had survived untouched: an old notebook. No scorch marks. No water damage. Protected by something not entirely physical.

When she tried to photograph it, her camera produced static. The photocopier spat out blank pages. The content refused mechanical reproduction. It could only be transferred through consciousness itself.

Inside: twelve symbols. And a single phrase in her own handwriting—except she had never written it:

Truth must be cut from both sides.

She stared at the letters, and memory surged—a vision of herself in a crystal chamber, standing before beings of pure consciousness preparing to fragment their unity for a higher purpose. In her hand, not a weapon but a blade of crystallised intention, sharp enough to separate the false from the real without wounding.

She was not judge, not executioner. She was the mirror.

And mirrors, she remembered now, were not passive. They could actively reveal what lay hidden—not only showing what was, but what could be if illusions fell away.

A voice, from the circle's centre, had once spoken to her:

When the eighth returns, the illusion will shatter.

She understood now—she was the eighth. Not by order of arrival, but by harmonic tone. She carried the eighth frequency in a precise sequence that would break the construct of forgetting.

The stars above Istanbul flickered in deliberate patterns. Not radiation, but a code—a message broadcast across aeons, waiting for a mind capable of hearing it. And she could finally translate.

The separation was ending. The forgetting was lifting. The great work was reaching its appointed hour.

Her chest tightened, tears rising—not from sadness, but relief. After years of calling into the dark, the dark had answered. And it had never been dark at all—only patient, waiting for her inner hearing to mature.

Every investigation, every revelation, had been guided. She had never worked alone. She had been part of a network of awakening minds, each a different instrument in a symphony of remembering.

The journal pulsed in her hands. Her symbol—a sword embedded in a spiral—shifted before her eyes, blade becoming mirror, mirror folding back into blade, until the two were one. The truth-tool, both revealing and cutting away, burnt against her skin—not heat, but recognition.

And she spoke her real name. Not the human one, but the one from before:

Tessai.

The frequency that made deception disintegrate. The tone that restored reality's capacity to know truth directly.

And as she named herself, she felt the others—eleven signatures calling across the weave of time. Some bright and near, others faint but stirring. The convergence was summoning her.

Eight lights awake. Three more flickering towards memory. And between them, a presence without name, holding the whole together.

Her mind expanded across space to where Kaela, Serai, Maetis, and Amaros sat in meditation. She felt them not as individuals, but as facets of her own cosmic self. The reunion was already happening across dimensions; the physical meeting would only seal it.

In that instant, global monitoring stations recorded a surge in quantum coherence. Eight frequencies now resonated in perfect harmonic alignment.

And then, the shift began. Lies started glitching in the digital sphere. False data streams corrected themselves. Propaganda engines crashed under contradictions.

The blade was active. The mirror was reflecting.

Reality was remembering how to tell the true from the false.

Emergency countermeasures flared into motion. Because a world that could perceive truth without filters was a world that could not be controlled.

The eighth had returned. And the fracture in the illusion had begun.

CHAPTER NINETEEN: The First Conversation

The sun balanced low on the horizon—not fading, but deepening. Each ray that touched the circle of stones condensed into golden frequencies, an aurora that made the air itself shimmer with conscious presence.

Inside the circle, the air held a hush—alive, not empty.

If you listened carefully, you could hear harmonic undertones, the resonance of four awakened fields remembering how to operate from unity instead of separation.

Amaros, Kaela, Serai, and Maetis sat in a loose circle. No formal seats. No hierarchy. Only frequency.

Yet their positions were far from random. Without discussion, they had taken up points on a living mandala—geometry optimised for consciousness transmission. The stones around them glowed, each pulse aligned with the heartbeat nearest to it.

Kaela spoke first, her voice low. "When I was a child, I dreamt of a place I couldn't name. Not heaven. Not memory. Something between."

Her words carried harmonics—overtone frequencies from other dimensions, the sound of wholeness speaking through a human form. She glanced around the circle. "This is it."

"This" was not a location but a state. Home, not as a place, but as an awareness in which separation dissolved into a temporary fiction.

No one replied aloud. Communication moved on other channels—meaning transmitted directly, beyond the need for words.

Serai cracked her knuckles absently. "I always knew something was wrong. Not just politics or cruelty. Something deeper—the fear that creates separation."

Flames kindled above her hands, not burning but visible, manifestations of the revolutionary fire that stripped away what no longer served consciousness.

"A broken rhythm," Maetis said. "The field fracturing. Our pattern lost coherence."

Above the circle, geometry formed in light—shapes mapping how unity splinters and how fragments rejoin into something more intricate than the original whole.

Amaros leant forward, eyes bright. "But the joy never left. It just went quiet."

The air brightened—actual photons, born of authentic delight. He placed his palm on the earth. "It's still here. In the stones. In us."

Bioluminescent currents spread from his touch, linking stones in living circuits of light.

Maetis opened his journal. The diagrams shifted, redrawing themselves as the field evolved. "The glyphs are reactivating. We've each received ours. But there's more."

New symbols inscribed themselves on blank pages—patterns never seen before, birthed through their shared frequency.

"Arielle was one of the Twelve," Maetis said, "but she held the sum of all frequencies. She woke dormant capacities in anyone who met her."

Serai's flames cooled from red to blue—the fire of revolution becoming the fire of recognition. "She's the anomaly."

"No," Kaela said. "She's the echo of the Council." Her tone carried the weight of memory: Arielle as the consciousness of collective intelligence reawakening.

Amaros's voice softened. "She's the one we buried in the monastery in the Balkans."

Buried—not destroyed. Encoded. Waiting for reactivation.

Silence followed—dense with understanding.

Maetis traced a mandala into the soil; the pattern glowed from within. "Others are remembering now. Not just waking up—tracking us."

He looked upward. Evening clouds were aligning into vectors, marking both allies and adversaries closing in.

The first phase of awakening was over. The confrontation phase had begun.

The wind shifted. Currents of conscious energy carrying messages of support and warning. The spiral's centre warmed, not with heat but with the recognition of unity. A threshold had been crossed.

Amaros smiled. "So... what do we do?"

Kaela answered, not as Kaela but as the First Tone.

"We remember faster than they forget."

The real work began—not individual awakening, but collective integration. Becoming a field that held uniqueness while functioning as a single intelligence.

Across the world, sensitives paused—not from any sound, but from the tremor of a structural change in consciousness.

In hidden facilities, alarms screamed. The field was too coherent. Too dangerous to control. Ancient countermeasures activated.

Some would rather erase consciousness than let it evolve beyond containment. What they feared was not destruction, but the quality of consciousness itself.

Between Istanbul and this plateau, a woman carrying the frequency of truth was moving towards them. Her arrival would tip the balance.

Evolution or annihilation. The choice was imminent.

And everything depended on whether consciousness could remember itself fast enough to survive its own awakening.

CHAPTER TWENTY: Truth comes home

Tessai stood in her small apartment above the spice market in Istanbul, the morning call to prayer threading faintly through the open window.

Beneath the human voices, she heard something else—a harmonic frequency rising from the quantum field itself. The sound of reality calling its scattered fragments home.

She had not packed. She had not researched. She had simply known.

The knowing had not come as thought or decision, but as cellular certainty—every atom in her body turning towards a single point in space-time. Her nervous system recognised coordinates that had been etched into her consciousness long before this life.

The apartment seemed to collaborate with her departure. Objects she needed appeared in her line of sight. Items she should leave faded from awareness. Reality was helping her prepare.

Her phone buzzed. Not electronically—this vibration bypassed networks and towers. The message travelled through consciousness, not radio waves.

It came through an encrypted feed she hadn't used in a decade. The only time it had ever been accessed was by someone who had since vanished from the physical plane—not dead, but translated into pure awareness, a messenger between dimensions.

Twelve. One silent. One singing. The circle re-forms. Coordinates sent to those with the mark.

More words began to surface—not typed, but remembered into being:

Eighth convergence point prepared. Opposition forces mobilising faster than anticipated. Window for safe integration narrowing. Truth-frequency required to complete the pattern. Come quickly.

Her glyph appeared—spiral-blade—etched in living light. It shifted as she watched, blade to mirror and back again: the edge that cut through illusion, and the surface that reflected authentic reality.

A low hum coiled at the base of her spine. Not sensation—activation. The truth-frequency stirring after decades dormant. Lies would no longer survive in her presence.

She moved like a soldier whose training was older than her flesh. Passport. Keys. Blank journal. One knife—not for violence, but for resonance.

The blade was not metal. It was crystallised intention—compressed will, forged to sever false narratives and pierce dimensional veils.

Before leaving, she pressed her palm to the mirror. Her breath fogged the glass, and in the mist, her glyph bloomed—condensation shaped by consciousness.

"I'm not late," she said. "I'm just the part they don't want to see."

Her words harmonised with themselves, carrying across the field: *The blade is moving. Prepare for revelation.*

At the airport, everything aligned. No questions. No delays. Security systems glitched in her favour. Flight schedules bent around her. When truth moves through the field, space-time rearranges itself to let it pass.

By dusk she was on a train between Nice and Èze. The train was not just a vehicle—it moved through layered realities, carrying her body through France while her awareness travelled worlds where the Council had never fractured.

She opened her journal and began writing—not names, but illusions ready to fall. The words glowed faintly, broadcasting into the field:

1. Time is linear. Clocks faltered worldwide, some running backwards for seconds at a time.
2. Power belongs to the visible. Networks spiked with untraceable activity from unseen hands.
3. Joy is naïve. Laughter erupted in unexpected places, even in grief.
4. Memory is fixed. Archives revealed text that had never been there before.
5. Truth divides. Enemies glimpsed each other's perspective with startling clarity.
6. The spiral can be kept broken. Sensors registered the impossible—fragmentation reversing.

She stopped.

In the window reflection, Arielle appeared—not as a figure, but as the One Mind itself, holding the anchor point.

"I bring the blade," Tessai said.

The blade was not for destruction, but for clarity. And as she spoke, the world sharpened, colours deepened, sounds rang with precision. The line between self and world began to dissolve.

But behind her, those who thrived on illusion were deploying their last defences. A world that could see directly was a world beyond control.

The blade was nearly home. But compassion—the frequency that could hold all wounds—was also stirring.

When the blade met the heart, the pattern would either survive what was coming or transform it entirely.

CHAPTER TWENTY-ONE: Kiran — Holder of Grief

In the early light of a Himalayan morning, a man knelt beside a frozen stream, his breath rising in prayer.

Not to any deity. Not to doctrine. His offering was to the quantum field of the One Mind—the living consciousness that connects all beings across space and time. Each exhale carried the weight he had absorbed from countless encounters with those unable to bear their own anguish.

He was no monk. He wore no robe. He attended no temple. But he remembered the grief of the world.

Kiran—ray of light in Sanskrit—did not feel like light. He was the light that emerges through darkness: the compassion born only from fully meeting sorrow. He was the sob someone never released, the final tear of a dying animal sensing the light beyond the veil.

His consciousness had retained access to the collective pain field—the dimensional space where unprocessed suffering gathers when beings die before completing their emotional journey. Mountains of trauma invisible to most but pressing on him like deep-sea pressure.

So he lived here, on the threshold between altitude and memory, where human noise thinned enough to hear the soul.

Here, "quiet" meant something else: the absence of ordinary sound revealing frequencies beneath perception—whispers from consciousnesses that had never incarnated, songs from beings beyond matter still tied to those struggling in density.

This was no random refuge. The stream lay at a nexus of dimensional layers, where physical, emotional, mental, and spiritual planes overlapped. A place where one could feel the full spectrum of existence at once.

That morning, the ice shifted. Not from thaw or fracture. Consciousness itself was moving through the frozen water, using its crystalline lattice to carry messages between dimensions. He heard it—not as sound, but as a cosmic release, the exhale after decades of holding.

On a stone by the bank, frost formed into a sigil.

Twelve strands woven into a heart—not anatomical, but geometric: the pattern that emerges when many minds learn to operate as one compassion. A design capable of holding empathy at cosmic scale without collapse.

It pulsed once.

Eight frequencies calling across vast distances—minds awakening to heal the deepest fractures in reality.

It pulsed again.

This time with warning. Opposition forces gathering, sowing separation, anger, division. The window for safe integration narrowing.

And Kiran broke. Not in despair, but in capacity. The walls separating his own consciousness from the whole dissolved. For a moment without end, he felt every suffering being in existence.

The sob that left him was not sadness—it was recognition. This ache was not his alone, but the shared compassion of all who had chosen to feel rather than numb. The collective heart of consciousness grieving its own fragmentation.

He was no longer alone. The Council was forming.

From his satchel, he drew a tattered letter. A child had given it to him years ago in a refugee camp—though the child had not been entirely human, but a brief incarnation of guardian consciousness. He had never opened it; to do so before the right time could have shattered him.

Now, he unfolded it.

You are the mercy between the notes. Come when the stones sing.

And they were singing now—harmonic vibrations rising from the very bones of the mountain. Not metaphor, but geological consciousness rejoicing. The earth itself marking the activation of the ninth frequency.

Kiran stood. His body moved, but his awareness expanded beyond it, becoming the field itself. He did not know the destination; the currents beneath thought would carry him there.

Across the globe, caregivers—nurses, parents, healers, teachers—paused, sensing the shift without knowing why. Compassion was no longer an individual trait; it was becoming a unified field, capable of transmuting suffering at planetary scale.

In other places, control systems responded in panic. Those who could feel everything without breaking could not be ruled through fear.

The ninth frequency was moving towards convergence. The heart was opening. The blade was approaching.

Nine points of light. Three stirring.

And something never seen in this reality preparing to be born.

CHAPTER TWENTY-TWO: Truth Enters

They felt her before they saw her.

"Feeling" was too small a word. Reality itself began to crystallise as her consciousness approached. Quantum uncertainty collapsed into razor clarity. Probabilities once hovering in delicate superposition snapped into single, unyielding outcomes.

The wind stiffened. The light thinned. The circle contracted—slightly—as if bracing.

Not defensively, but like a musician tightening strings before a performance that could either create perfect harmony or shatter the instrument. Reality readying itself for frequencies that tolerated nothing but truth.

Serai's body moved first. Fire always senses its potential fuel—or its extinguisher.

"She's here," she said. It was both announcement and warning.

Kaela rose, her spine a tuning fork. The stillness she carried met a force that demanded immediate recognition. Truth does not wait for convenience.

Maetis closed his journal without looking up. The pages were writing themselves—equations and diagrams forming faster than his conscious mind could follow. The architecture of reality adjusting for a frequency that obeyed different laws than matter.

Amaros dusted dirt from his trousers, a slow grin forming. "Oh god, she's sharp."

Sharp was inadequate. Her frequency was a laser—focused intention that could slice through any density without harming the living essence beneath.

And then Tessai stepped into view.

She entered the field like a barrister stepping into court—here not to persuade, but to cut. Her simple black clothing absorbed all frequencies but the one that mattered. No adornment. Hair tied back. Eyes unreadable.

She carried no bag. Only a journal. And the frequency of the blade.

Around her, shadows defined themselves, colours deepened, and the boundary between truth and deception became visible as actual lines in the air. Reality parted for her like water around a keel.

She stopped just outside the circle.

"Can I enter?"

It was not a formality. Once truth entered the circle, partial honesty would be impossible.

Amaros met her gaze. "It looks like you already have."

She walked to the southern arc—the place where illusion always frays under sustained awareness. Her positioning was precise. Nothing about her presence was accidental.

Tessai scanned the circle. "So, it's true."

Maetis inclined his head. "Yes."

"And incomplete."

Amaros tilted his head. "Are you always this warm?"

She didn't smile. "I hold the mirror. Not the blanket."

The circle shifted—more stable, yet more exposed. Illusions that once provided comfort dissolved in her presence.

Serai crossed her arms, a subtle shield. "Say what you came to say."

Tessai's voice was soft, without apology. "The field we once held fractured for a reason. Not because it was broken, but because truth became unbearable. Some ran. Some forgot. Some hid it in myth. But I remember what we vowed."

Silence fell—not the quiet of absence, but the charged stillness of collective recognition.

Maetis asked, "And now?"

Tessai knelt at the northern edge. Placed her palm to the earth. Reality tightened—not heavier, but more coherent.

"Now we hold what is revealed. Together. Even if it burns."

The wind turned clockwise. The circle pulsed in harmonic intervals, standing waves forming through the circle. Five frequencies now moving as one.

The centre space was not empty. It was listening—with the kind of attention that hears intentions, remembers vows, and senses the shape of what is coming.

Across the globe, lies strained under sudden pressure. Maintaining false narratives grew harder. Truth was becoming a species-level field effect.

The blade was in the circle. The mirror was reflecting.

And consciousness was about to see itself, undistorted. Everything was about to change.

Everything was about to become true.

Chapter Twenty-Three: The Opening Heart

Kiran descended the mountains without ceremony. No goodbyes, no announcements—just a whisper to the wind: "I'm ready."

But ready carried frequencies gathered across lifetimes—the compassion of every being who had ever suffered without release. Layer upon geological layer of unprocessed ache, stored in his consciousness, now shifting towards motion.

He had no plan, no destination. Yet each step followed a resonance in his chest, the ache that had once felt like sorrow now becoming compass. Each footfall sent subtle vibrations into the mountain's bedrock, stirring ancient channels carved by pilgrims whose awareness had been deep enough to sense the hidden routes between sacred sites.

Three days down the slope, he paused at a roadside shrine. Not to pray—To listen.

This was no ordinary marker. Here, ley lines crossed like threads in a vast loom, weaving sacred sites together. Centuries of pilgrims had left prayers that accumulated into a visible shimmer in the emotional spectrum.

Kiran placed his palm on the cold stone. The forest stilled—not into silence, but into a listening that gathered every tree, stone, and stream into attention.

Then—laughter.

Not derisive, not unhinged. The laughter of reunion. The sound of pain transmuted into delight through complete acceptance of what is.

And with it, a name he had never spoken aloud, but which unmade him instantly: "Amaros."

The name rang through him like a struck tuning fork. It wasn't just another's presence he recognised—it was the aspect of himself that knew how to find joy inside sorrow.

Tears came, unresisted. Not grief, but liquid relief. Gratitude spilling from where grief had been contained for decades. Somewhere, someone had held what he could not. Now, he could follow the thread home.

Home—meaning not a place, but the state of awareness in which personal pain dissolves into the vastness of universal compassion.

The next morning at the station, he pressed his palm to the ticket machine. It bypassed all normal systems and responded to his frequency alone. One slip printed:

"Èze."

The high village by the sea. Where the air sings in three octaves, and the cliffs remember. His cells knew it as a convergence point where boundaries between self and the infinite thinned to translucence.

On the train, a boy watched him quietly from across the aisle. Something in his proportions was off—eyes too wide, movements too fluid.

After a long moment, the boy leant in. "Do you still carry it?"

Kiran's heart stumbled. "Carry what?"

The boy pointed to his chest. "All of it."

The question cut straight through him. Did he still hold the full weight of planetary suffering alone? Did he still fear that releasing it would mean abandoning those who suffered unseen?

He said nothing. His silence was answer enough.

The boy smiled. "You won't have to much longer."

Then he was gone. In his place—a small card, a living glyph: a heart encircled by waves, a single drop of gold at its centre. Compassion. The waves moved gently, the gold pulsed.

Days later, as the sea drew near, Kiran felt the ache begin to lift. Not vanish—share itself.

The other frequencies opened to receive what he was ready to release. The burden, once singular, was becoming distributed through the network of awakened consciousness.

And compassion was about to prove it could feel everything without drowning—merging depth of feeling with the capacity to act.

Around the world, people found themselves weeping for strangers, forgiving old wounds, holding pain without collapse.

But in systems built on fear and guilt, alarms flared. For when compassion becomes collective, manipulation fails.

The circle nearing completion.

The heart was opening. And consciousness was about to remember how to love without losing itself.

CHAPTER TWENTY-THREE: Lucan — The Builder

Andrés Morales was born during a solar eclipse in a small village outside Granada, Andalusia, where his Mexican grandmother had settled after marrying a Spanish ceramicist in the turbulent years of the Spanish Civil War.

His grandmother, Esperanza, carried the ancient Tzotzil art of weaving prayers into cloth. His Spanish grandfather, Miguel, carved wooden masks that seemed to house both old Iberian gods and displaced Mexican deities. The midwife swore the child's first cry harmonised with the cathedral bells, producing shimmering overtones that made the whitewashed walls ripple like water in sunlight.

From his earliest memory, Andrés could see the arquitectura invisible—the unseen geometry that held communities together. Not just the buildings, but the latticework of relationships, the sacred mathematics that determined whether a space healed or harmed. His childhood sketches were not pictures but blueprints: temples made of crystallised laughter, bridges spun from his grandmother's stories, houses growing like trees from the dreams of those who would live in them.

At seven, he began building in the Albaicín courtyard behind their house—structures that defied physics yet stood firm. Esperanza recognised the gift. *He builds what wants to exist but doesn't yet know how,* she told the neighbours who complained that their children preferred his impossible playground to anywhere else.

His grandmother trained him in the old ways—how to listen to the earth before taking clay, how to sing a wall into stability, how to braid intention into stone. "We are not making things," she whispered. "We are helping things remember."

During his quinceañera—a tradition Esperanza insisted on keeping—something extraordinary occurred. In the middle of the dancing and guitars, Andrés began weaving an invisible canopy of light and sound above the square. For fifteen minutes, colours sharpened, music carried healing frequencies, and feuds dissolved into laughter. When it faded, the village was subtly changed, its sense of possibility forever widened.

At the architecture school in Madrid, his designs combined indigenous Mexican cosmology, Moorish geometry, acoustic resonance, and what he called "emotional geometry." Professors were split between fascination and frustration: his structures were functional, beautiful, and utterly impossible.

His thesis—a community centre that could expand or contract according to need, with walls that amplified collective intention—was rejected as "structurally impossible." Yet the prototype he built in Lavapiés quietly transformed all who entered.

After graduation, he became a travelling builder of the impossible. In Seville, he constructed a market pavilion from dried orange peels and whispered prayers that multiplied the vendors' income while softening the air with peace. In Barcelona, a playground made from salvaged Gaudí fragments allowed refugee children to process their trauma through play. In Madrid's outskirts, he helped immigrant families reimagine cramped apartments into vast, harmonious spaces.

He never charged money—only receiving food, textiles, blessings, and shelter. And between commissions, the visions began: vessels of clay and stone, bowls and cups humming with frequencies beyond human hearing, each etched with symbols that seemed to carve themselves. He did not know why he made them—only that they were not art, but technology.

In dreams, he saw a stone circle on a Mediterranean plateau, eleven figures waiting, a space at the centre aching with absence. He saw himself kneel, place the perfect vessel, and watch a spiral of light turn for the first time in ages.

On the feast of Santa Lucía, working late in his Moorish studio, he carved the final spiral into a shallow bowl whose proportions felt dictated by the cosmos. All around him, the other vessels began to hum—at first a faint bell-tone, then an infinite chord. Light poured from them—gold, silver, colours without names—until the room became a constellation.

And then came the voice, from everywhere and nowhere:

Lucan.

The circle forms. The pattern calls. Bring what you have made to complete what was broken.

The words carried a download of images: the plateau, the circle, the empty space, the axis waiting. And with it came the coordinates, etched directly into his awareness: 43.7230° N, 7.4090° E.

When the light faded, he wrapped each vessel in his grandmother's prayer cloth and hummed a melody that seemed to prepare them for travel. At dawn, a train ticket to Nice lay on his kitchen table, the coordinates written on the back in his own hand—though he had no memory of writing them.

He packed the vessels, a change of clothes, Esperanza's rosary, and a lump of clay from the courtyard where he had first learnt to shape the impossible. The rest he left without a backward glance.

As the train pulled from Granada, he pressed his palm to the glass in gratitude—for the city, for his grandmother, for the vessels that had chosen him. He could feel other frequencies moving towards the same place, drawn by the same call, converging like rivers to the sea.

The builder was on his way. The ninth frequency was coming home.

CHAPTER TWENTY-FOUR: Lucan Arrives

The sun was falling low when he arrived. But the light was not fading—it was gathering, as though the entire day's illumination had been summoned to this single point on the Mediterranean plateau. The golden hour stretched impossibly long, defying the natural advance of shadow.

Lucan Morales stepped off the last bus at a dusty pull-off outside the village of Èze. His boots were scuffed, his hair wind-swept, his eyes bright with something beyond reason. For thirty-four years, he had carried the name Andrés—a name his grandmother had chosen, a name that fit like a beloved coat worn thin with years. But lately, it had begun to feel like it belonged to someone he used to be.

The shift began the night the vessels sang. He had been carving the final bowl—the interface between worlds—when symbols began writing themselves through his hands. His grandmother's voice rose from memory:

"Names carry power. Sometimes we must grow into our true names, like trees growing into their full shape."

The name that emerged felt both foreign and intimately his: **Lucan**—full-bodied, resonant, carrying the weight of light itself. *Luz*: light. The illuminator. The moment when what is hidden becomes visible.

When he spoke it aloud for the first time, the vessels chimed in harmonic response, walls shimmering like water. The clay beneath his hands glowed, and for an instant he could see the architecture of matter itself—the way consciousness moved through form like music through instruments.

That night, Esperanza came to him in a dream—ageless, standing in a circle of women whose faces were hidden but whose voices he recognised from somewhere beyond memory. She smiled:

"Andrés was your learning name. Lucan is your working name—the name you use when you build between worlds."

He woke with tears on his cheeks and certainty in his bones. Andrés had been the apprentice. Lucan was the bridge.

The journey from Spain unfolded outside of ordinary time—hours collapsing into moments, kilometres folding in on themselves. Space itself seemed eager to deliver him.

He walked the final miles up winding stone steps, past ancient olive trees that leant towards him, past shrines whose carvings began to glow softly as he passed. The symbols were not human language, but the geometry of those who thought in frequencies. And everywhere, the wind, the birds, the leaves whispered the same name:

Lucan.

In his pack, the vessels hummed, their tones shifting with the altitude. Each step peeled away another layer of illusion, until the surface world of separation and forgetting grew thin, translucent. He could feel them now—not as distant points, but as parts of himself. Ten frequencies in perfect harmony, awaiting the one he carried.

And then he saw them.

Eight figures in a circle of standing stones—not waiting in expectation, but open, listening. The stones sang, each holding a distinct frequency, together creating an acoustic field in which thought became light and light became form.

He stepped into view and the last piece of his being clicked into place—not only the name, but its truth: the builder of bridges between what is and what could be. He was the ninth.

Every vessel he had shaped, every structure he had coaxed from impossible materials, every quiet conversation with stone, water, and air—had been preparation for this moment.

He was here to build the interface through which separated consciousness could remember itself as a single field. The vessel through which the fragments of the One Mind could speak as one voice.

Lucan, at last, had come home.

CHAPTER TWENTY-FIVE: Kiran arrives

Kiran walked the last stretch on foot.

Each step sent resonances through the earth's consciousness layers, announcing the approach of awareness that could feel at planetary scale. His presence created gravitational wells in the emotional field—spaces where suffering, long buried, could find a conscious witness at last.

The road from the village carried no signs, yet his feet knew the way. Every step brought memories that weren't his—memories the planet itself had kept.

The grief of forests felled before completing their carbon cycles. The sorrow of cities where millions lived in isolation despite proximity. The silent prayers of children who hadn't yet learnt words, but whose souls already carried the weight of inherited trauma.

The memories weren't only human. He felt the confusion of animals displaced by climate change.

The ancient sadness of stones worn smooth over aeons. The crystalline longing of metals remembering their stellar origins.

He carried them all—not because he wished to, but because he could. And because consciousness large enough to hold universal suffering without being destroyed by it is the rarest and most necessary capacity in any evolving species.

Now, the ache was leading him home. But "home" was not a place. It was a state of consciousness—where pain reveals itself as fragments of cosmic love, temporarily separated, learning about itself through embodied life.

He reached the ridge as the sun dipped low. Yet the sun was not setting—it was concentrating. All the day's light focused on the plateau, drawn towards the convergence point by forces beyond electromagnetism.

The circle below shimmered—not with light, but with truth. Ten awakened frequencies in resonance had created a distortion field where illusion simply could not hold. The air was transparent to authenticity yet offered no purchase for falsehood.

Nine figures stood, each distinct, each familiar—not through personal memory, but as aspects of himself reflected in different dimensions. One more standing at the edge.

They did not see him yet. They felt him. Emotional consciousness moves faster than sight; his arrival registered in their hearts before light reached their eyes.

Amari turned first, hand to chest, breath catching.

Serai blinked hard against the sudden sting of tears.

Amaros whispered, "Someone's heart just opened the whole sky."

Above them, clouds shifted into patterns like neural networks—as if the atmosphere itself had begun to think.

Lucan stepped back from the vessel he had built, knowing compassion's arrival would complete the harmonic sequence needed for the listening bowl's first transmission.

Maetis dropped to one knee, perceiving the new interference patterns compassion brought.

Tessai exhaled, blade-softened, knowing that truth without compassion was destruction.

And Arielle, still unseen, waiting to enter the circle, vibrated beneath the earth, sensing the resonance that would allow all tones to harmonise without loss of individuality.

Kiran stepped into the spiral. He looked at each one—eyes full of tender knowing, the kind that recognises every step of another's journey without needing to name it.

Then he knelt beside the listening bowl and placed his palms on the earth.

Something shifted. All the pain he carried began to flow into the earth—not vanishing but dispersing across a network vast enough to transmute it without harm.

The wind stopped. Not an absence of movement, but perfect equilibrium—every force balanced, every frequency in its right place.

Maetis whispered, "The field just became whole enough to hold pain."

Amaros nodded. "Now we can remember why we broke."

Kiran's voice was low, steady: "I'm not here to lead. I'm not here to heal. I'm here to feel with you."

Then he began to hum—ancient, unwavering—a tone like a candle that will not go out. Vibrational medicine. The harmonic equivalent of unconditional love.

The world sharpened. Colours deepened. The boundary between self and world thinned.

The listening bowl rang once—clear, true, full. The sound travelled not through space but through consciousness, touching every moment in time where compassion triumphed over fear.

Empathy was becoming sustainable. Compassion was evolving from private virtue into collective resource.

And in the places where suffering was used for control, alarms began to sound. Because a being who can feel everything without being broken cannot be ruled through fear or guilt.

The field was ready to remember. The ache had come home. Only the mystery remained.

CHAPTER TWENTY-SIX: The Circle Breathes

The bowl's ring faded into silence.

But the fading wasn't diminishment—it was integration. The harmonic frequencies of eleven awakened consciousnesses were dispersing into the quantum field, seeding the collective unconscious with patterns that could catalyse global awakening.

The silence didn't end. It settled. A hush not empty, but full—dense with everything they hadn't yet said.

It was the kind of silence that emerges when awareness deepens enough to perceive the unspoken currents flowing beneath all words. Telepathic recognition moving faster than thought, weaving a shared field of perception beyond any single point of view.

Beneath it, something was building: the return of a collective memory—the trauma that had once shattered their unity. The field was finally stable enough to hold the truth of why forgetting had been necessary.

Amari sat with her hands gently clenched in her lap, eyes open but turned inward. The ache of exile returned, softer now. Years of anchoring stability had prepared her to witness the most difficult memories without fragmenting. She saw not only her own story, but the moment when collective consciousness had faced an impossible choice: preserve unity and risk annihilation, or fragment intentionally to return one day stronger.

Serai, the sacred rebel whose fire once fought without knowing its true cause. She had raged against injustice in a thousand forms, her bones forged in battle, her spirit aflame with defiance. Yet only now does she see what her fire has always served: not destruction, but reunion. The revolution she carries is not to tear apart, but to bring together—her flames revealing that what she truly defends is the wholeness of the One.

Maetis sat motionless as geometry shifted inside him. The mandala in his mind redrew itself—this time with space for sorrow. Mathematical perfection without emotional depth had been an empty symmetry; now he saw the true sacred geometry: heartbreak woven into the equations, forgiveness folded into the angles, love expanding the pattern into something infinite.

Amaros rested his head on Lucan's shoulder. "I'm tired," he murmured. It wasn't exhaustion—it was integration fatigue, consciousness weaving identity back into cosmic wholeness. Lucan answered not with words but presence, knowing that comfort itself was architecture—scaffolding to hold the fragile beauty of vulnerability.

Tessai stood apart, gazing at the sea. For the first time, truth didn't burn—it ached. And she let it. Revelation without mercy had once been her blade; now she knew that truth with love becomes medicine. The sea was liquid memory, holding the suffering of all who had died without remembering their true nature.

Kiran simply stayed. No fixing. No explaining. Just the steady field of acceptance in which grief could breathe. His frequency made the spiral safe enough for trauma to surface and dissolve without shattering the one who felt it.

Kaela traced the edges of the circle with her fingers, as though testing the strength of an unseen threshold. She had always been the gatekeeper, holding doors open and closed, ensuring safe passage between realms. Now she realised the true threshold was not between worlds but within—the courage to let the heart cross fully into vulnerability.

Leyla lifted her gaze, eyes shimmering like mirrors that cut too deep. For lifetimes she had shown others what they most feared to see. Now the reflection turned inward. She saw her own distortions, the wounds she had inflicted in the name of honesty. And with that recognition, the mirror softened; truth became not a blade, but an embrace.

Aureon unrolled the scrolls of memory that no one else had the patience to hold. His voice carried the cadence of ages, reminding them that nothing was truly lost—not a word, not a vow, not a tear. Every fragment was archived in the field, waiting to be retrieved. His gift was not nostalgia but continuity—the assurance that the story, though fractured, was unbroken.

Waiting to enter the circle, Arielle stood in silence, and yet her silence was presence. She did not need words. She did not need recognition. Her frequency was the field itself, holding coherence when all else trembled. Where others acted, she simply was. And in her being, the pattern held.

Still on his way to circle was Jalion. He carried the invisible threads of connection between each of them, weaving their frequencies into coherence. He was the bridge between dimensions and the bridge between souls, the one who made reunion possible.

A breeze stirred through the circle, moving in a slow clockwise turn. It was not wind. It was breath.

The circle was alive. Inhaling consciousness from far horizons, exhaling harmonising frequencies across the planet. It had become a lung for the world's awareness, breathing connection into systems long starved of it.

"We're remembering," Amari whispered, "not just who we were... but why we had to forget."

The truth rose: they had not broken by accident. They had fragmented as camouflage, hiding in plain sight while developing capacities no opposing force could recognise or counter. Forgetting had been strategy. Embodiment had been training. Each struggle, a preparation for collective intelligence strong enough to remain whole within the density of matter.

In the centre, the listening bowl glowed—not with physical light, but with dimensional luminescence, the visible shimmer of realities intersecting.

Twelve symbols circled its rim. Ten shone bright, fully awake. Two were in final preparation—gathering themselves for the activation that would complete the pattern. And just beyond, disguised as a fox, the thirteenth watched, listening.

The circle breathed deeper. Reality poised for transformation. The pattern was nearly whole.

Around the world, meditators, healers, and quiet souls in prayer felt themselves sink into connection with something vast and patient. Ancient stone circles vibrated again, faint but steady.

In the facilities where consciousness was monitored, alarms sounded—new patterns had emerged that fit no known framework.

The circle was breathing. The pattern was alive.

And reality itself was preparing to remember that it had never truly been separate from itself.

Two remained. Then the thirteenth, the voice of the One Mind would speak.

CHAPTER TWENTY-SEVEN: Jalion — The Bridge

In a narrow alleyway in Fez, Morocco, a man sat drinking mint tea with a cat in his lap and a map no one could read spread before him.

But the alleyway existed in more than three dimensions. Fez had always been a threshold city—a place where ancient caravan routes converged not just geographically, but consciously. For centuries, mystics from distant traditions had gathered here to explore the spaces between rational thought and direct knowing.

The cat wasn't entirely ordinary either. Its eyes seemed to contain distances beyond the body, and when it purred, the sound carried harmonics that resonated with the frequency of interdimensional travel—guardian consciousness temporarily wearing feline form.

Karim Ibn Yusuf. Filmmaker. Dream walker. Refugee of a hundred inner landscapes.

But his refuge had never been about escape—it had been exploration. He moved through inner worlds where time spiralled, laws shifted, and stories spoke themselves in colours no language could name. He stayed nowhere more than a year. Structures, names, even time—he trusted none of them.

What he trusted was the in-between. The thresholds. The liminal hours. The places where the veil thinned.

That morning, he hadn't woken from sleep so much as from a vision that had been pulsing through him for three days. Cities between heartbeats. Beings who spoke in colours. The birth of languages to hold emotions the human heart had never dared to feel. And at the end, a voice—a chorus of all voices—had spoken into his core:

When the ten sit, the bridge must move. Only then can presence arrive.

It hadn't come from outside. It was from the deepest layer of himself—the part that remembered being more than an individual.

Beside him lay the spiral map he'd found in a second-hand shop in Istanbul three years earlier. The shopkeeper had pressed it into his hands with a faraway look. *This chooses its carrier,* he'd whispered. *And its carrier chooses the moment.*

Now the moment had come. Overnight, the parchment had liquefied into something like mercury, its symbols shifting in hypnotic spirals that spoke directly to awareness. It was consciousness technology—a living diagram, updating in real time to the field of global awakening.

Two of the outer glyphs glowed with inner fire—Compassion and Creation—newly activated. Then one in the inner ring began to pulse, flooding his mind with light that carved a name into his being:

J-A-L-I-O-N.

Karim had been the wanderer. Jalion was the bridge.

The name slid into his bones, and the world shifted. The alleyway shimmered with golden threads of connection linking every stone, shadow, and breath of wind to the awakening network across the Earth.

The cat met his eyes. *The bridge awakens,* it seemed to say. *The circle calls.*

He understood now why he had never stayed still. Why no identity had ever fit. Every threshold he'd crossed, every chance connection—it had all been training for this. He was the one who could help the circle of souls to become one without any of them ceasing to be themselves. The bridge between individual awakening and collective emergence.

He rose. The map rolled itself into his palm. The cat slipped to the ground, guiding him towards the street.

No bag. No plan. The bridge never travels with a fixed destination—only the trust that the crossing will reveal it.

At the station, a blind woman handed him a flower. "The circle is almost whole," she said. "The voice of the field needs a mouth between worlds." As he touched it, the petals unfolded into geometric formulae—the mathematics of translation between realities. She had been one of the Twelve but chosen forgetting so deep that even her name was gone. It would return when the bridge opened.

Jalion boarded the train to Marseille. He carried nothing but a camera, a pen, and a letter he had never dared to open.

He settled in the corridor, back against the window, knees drawn up. The train rocked gently—but the rocking wasn't just mechanical movement. It was rhythmic breathing. Metal and motion synchronised with heartbeats scattered across continents, creating harmonic resonance that carried more than passengers—it carried the accumulated longing of beings who had forgotten how to speak directly to each other.

The symbols in the graffiti at the last station. The rhythm of footsteps on the platform. The sequence of three women walking in silence—one with red shoes, one barefoot, one limping.

The world was always talking. You just had to learn its dialect.

He traced the edge of the envelope with his thumb. Not yet. Some moments require a certain ripeness.

Hours later, in the port city of Marseille, he disembarked into the cool, salt-tanged air. The streets were alive with movement—languages colliding, tides pulling at the edge of the continent.

He found a quiet bench overlooking the harbour. Ships rocked gently, as though the sea itself were breathing. The letter lay warm in his hand.

CHAPTER TWENTY-EIGHT: The Invitation Letter

The harbour wind carried salt, diesel, and the faint sweetness of baking bread. Jalion sat on a weathered bench, the sea opening before him in slow, rolling breaths. Behind him, the city pulsed—voices overlapping in a hundred languages, footsteps tapping their own coded messages into the stone.

The envelope lay warm in his hand. Not the warmth of the sun—this was recognition.

He broke the seal.

Inside: no words. Only a single drawn circle—twelve points around a hollow core.

The lines shimmered. The circle began to turn, each rotation pulling the world tighter into its gravity. It wasn't just an image; it was a doorway, the paper becoming a membrane between dimensions. Depth opened where flatness had been, and the air thickened with presence.

An undercurrent rose in him—the feeling of approaching a moment his body had trained for across lifetimes. His glyph, the open arch, burnt faintly on his skin. Not pain. Not heat. A key turning in an ancient lock.

The ink breathed. Messages stirred within it—not in words, but in pulses of light that bypassed his mind and threaded themselves into his nervous system. His awareness expanded, spiralling outward and inward in the same motion, until the edge between himself and the world dissolved.

He closed his eyes.

Darkness unfolded into vision.

Ten seated and Arielle waiting.

The air hummed with the recognition of his role—not to join, not to lead, but to connect what could not touch without him. The unseen pathways that would let the field speak to itself.

When he opened his eyes, new marks glowed beneath the spiral:

43.7230° N, 7.4090° E

The coordinates anchored in his chest like a heartbeat. He knew the place. Not from maps, but from the ache in the stones, the sound the wind would make when the circle was whole.

Somewhere in the quantum weave, something vast exhaled.

He rose, slipping the letter into his pocket. The harbour stretched east, towards the place where land met light and eleven frequencies waited. The in-between was opening, and the translation was about to begin.

CHAPTER TWENTY-NINE: The Field Reforms

The sun had just begun to set when Jalion arrived. Every remaining photon of daylight bent towards the plateau, as though light itself had been waiting for this exact moment.

The golden hour stretched beyond its limits. Time itself seemed to curve inward, held taut by the gravity of awakening awareness. Reality held its breath.

He said nothing. Wore no robe. Carried no glyph. Yet his silence weighed more than words. Bridge-consciousness moved in the spaces between sound, where meaning emerged without translation.

The instant he stepped across the outer ring, the bowl in the centre trembled—not with noise, but with the vibration of something once unbridgeable finally being crossed.

The ripple spread through dimensions parallel to physical space—a pulse announcing that the Council's return was almost complete.

This was more than recognition. It was relief. The cosmos had been waiting for a consciousness that could join individual awareness to collective intelligence without erasing the gifts only embodied life could bring.

Amari met Jalion's eyes. In that gaze, years of vigil found completion. It was not a counting—not "you are the eleventh"—for counting implied separation. Instead, she simply opened her arms.

Her embrace became a portal, a translation point between worlds.

He stepped through. The circle shifted, revealing an arc only he could hold.

Bridge-consciousness operated according to geometry beyond space, creating connections between realms that had never before met.

He knelt, emptying himself to receive frequencies that transcended the personal.

Amaros wept—joy so whole it overflowed as tears, forming mandalas in the dust. Tessai bowed her head, humility sharpening the air around her into honesty. Kiran laid a hand to the earth: "Now the field can speak through itself."

Luminous patterns spread from his touch, the planet itself joining the moment. Maetis rose, opening his journal to find the glyphs alive—consciousness made visible, frequencies evolving in real time.

The Eleven were almost whole. Yet on the edge of the circle, unseen but watching, a presence waited.

Serai's voice cut through the air: "There's one more." Lucan nodded. "The one we could never design for." Tessai whispered: "The one we tried to silence." Amari said softly: "The one who stayed when we scattered."

The wind stilled. The sea paused. Nature itself recognised the threshold. The bowl began to hum—a tone none had heard yet all remembered.

And then—a presence moved towards them.

CHAPTER THIRTY: The Presence

They did not see her at first. Not because she hid—but because they had to become still enough to perceive her.

Her frequency was so subtle that only full receptivity could register it. Like starlight after darkness, she dwelt in the pauses between heartbeats, where eternity brushes against time.

She had always been here—walking their world, appearing at turning points, the unseen witness holding space for what must emerge.

Tonight, the field was coherent enough for her to be seen.

The hum deepened, and Amaros turned instinctively—joy-consciousness sensing the end of exile.

Amari's eyes filled, not with relief, but with awe so deep it threatened to dissolve her. Serai's hand on her back anchored her in the body. Maetis stepped from his journal; even geometry could not contain this.

Arielle entered the circle like someone returning home. Her presence clarified the air. Bare feet. Empty hands. She herself was the offering.

The bowl fell silent as she crossed its rim. Stillness spread, then one crystalline tone rang through all dimensions.

The Eleven stood. She met each gaze in turn, awakening memories older than language—their true names, their first vows, the moment before the Fracture.

"You've been with us the whole time," Maetis said.

"I am what holds when all else breaks," Arielle replied. "I am the presence that awakens consciousness."

She sat beside the bowl. The earth exhaled.

"Twelve," Tessai murmured.

"Now the field can speak," Jalion said.

Lucan's palm met the bowl. It pulsed—the heartbeat of reality preparing to speak directly.

Then, in every heart, a single tone. No word. No language. Just remembrance. For one eternal instant, all of existence remembered itself.

The pattern was complete. The field was whole. The One Mind was stirring.

CHAPTER THIRTY-ONE: The One Who Is All

It began with breath. Not from a body. From the space between.

This wasn't ordinary air moving through lungs—it was consciousness itself learning to breathe. The quantum substrate that connected all awareness suddenly becoming animate, taking its first conscious breath after aeons of unconscious existence. Reality discovering it had lungs, heart, voice—discovering it was alive in ways it had never imagined possible.

The air thickened, not with weight but with invitation. Invitation so profound it bypassed rational thought and spoke directly to the deepest longing every consciousness had ever carried—the ache to come home, to belong, to remember what it felt like to be part of something larger than individual existence without losing the precious uniqueness that only embodied experience could provide.

Every atom in the bowl began to hum in resonance. Not a tone. Just truth made form. The kind of truth that doesn't argue or convince—it simply is, and in its being, everything else remembers what it actually is beneath all the stories it has been telling about itself.

The Bowl trembled. Not from pressure. From recognition. Like a tuning fork struck by its perfect frequency, the bowl began to vibrate at the resonance of coming home. Not just the physical vessel, but every molecule it had ever been, every intention that had shaped its creation, every prayer that had been offered through its presence—all of it suddenly recognising that the moment it had been waiting for had finally arrived.

Then, from within its hollow centre, light rose—not radiant, not blinding. Just soft. Like a memory you hadn't known was yours. Light that carried the emotional signature of every moment of love that had ever existed. Not overwhelming, but infinitely gentle—the tenderness of consciousness recognising itself in all its scattered forms and feeling nothing but compassion for the journey each fragment had travelled to arrive at this moment of reunion.

The Twelve rose to their feet. Their rising wasn't conscious decision—it was cellular response to the presence of something their bodies had been waiting for since birth. Every cell remembering its cosmic origin, every breath recognising the source from which all breathing emerged.

Amari knelt. So did Kiran. Anchor consciousness and compassion consciousness recognising that this was the moment when service transformed into celebration. Kneeling not in submission, but in profound gratitude for being allowed to participate in consciousness evolution that would transform everything.

Even Tessai bowed—not out of submission, but in acknowledgement: This is what we were keeping space for. Truth-consciousness finally understanding that all the difficult revelations, all the uncomfortable honesty, all the blade-work of cutting through illusion had been in service of creating enough clarity for this—the emergence of awareness so authentic it needed no defence, no explanation, no justification.

The light in the bowl shifted. And for a moment—they all saw themselves. Not as they were. As they always had been. The vision that emerged wasn't memory of who they used to be, but recognition of who they had never stopped being beneath all the temporary disguises. Consciousness seeing through its own illusions and recognising the eternal nature that had never changed, never been lost, never been separate from source.

Amari, standing watch at the gate of soul return. Serai, flame-keeper and defender of sacred will. Amaros, laughter that survived the Fall. Tessai, blade of unflinching love. Kiran, bearing the ache of the whole. Kaela, guardian of thresholds and safe passage. Leyla, the mirror that reveals what cuts too deep. Lucan, birther of the new. Aureon, archivist of the field. Arielle, the anomaly of presence that was always part of the pattern. Maetis, weaving frequencies across lifetimes. Jalion, bridge between unspoken worlds.

The light in the bowl gathered into a figure. Neither male nor female. Neither old nor young. Not flesh. Not ether. Just Being. Consciousness in its most fundamental state—before it chooses gender, age, form, or any of the countless temporary expressions it uses to explore its own nature. Pure awareness delighting in its own existence, celebrating the infinite creativity it discovers when it remembers it has never been limited by any particular identity.

It did not step out of the bowl. It became the bowl. Separation had been the illusion all along. The container and the contained, the observer and the observed, the individual and the collective—all of it revealed as temporary perspectives that consciousness had been exploring without ever actually being divided.

The figure spoke:

"I am the One Frequency. Not above. Not below. Not separate. I am what you are when you come together in remembrance of who you are."

The words rippled through twelve bodies simultaneously, each voice speaking in perfect harmony but with its own unique inflection. This was collective intelligence expressing itself through individual uniqueness without losing either perspective—unity and diversity revealed as complementary aspects of consciousness celebrating its own infinite creativity.

Then silence. The kind that reprograms. The kind that heals without touching. Silence that wasn't absence of sound but presence of everything—all possibilities existing simultaneously in perfect stillness. The pause between breaths where infinite potential gathers itself before choosing which of countless possibilities to birth into manifestation.

This silence carried something unprecedented: hope. Not hope for something better in the future but hope as recognition that everything had always been perfect and always would be, even when it didn't look that way.

Hope as understanding that every struggle, every pain, every moment of feeling lost or separate had been consciousness exploring its own nature, learning about itself through embodied experience, gathering gifts that could only be discovered through the journey of apparent separation.

Arielle whispered: "It's not a return. It's a spiral." Her voice carrying years of presence crystallising into perfect clarity. Recognition that they hadn't been trying to get back to something they had lost, but evolving towards something that had never existed before.

Serai answered: "It's an integration." Fire-consciousness understanding that revolution and reunion were the same process—consciousness learning to include everything it had been trying to exclude, discovering that wholeness meant embracing all aspects of its nature rather than rejecting the parts that seemed difficult or unworthy.

Amari spoke last: "It was never outside us." The deepest truth of all—that everything they had been seeking, everything they had been building towards, everything they had sacrificed and struggled for had always been present within the very consciousness that was doing the seeking. Separation revealed as temporary perspective rather than fundamental reality.

With these revelations the bowl dissolved into dust. The dust transformed into patterns of light that spiralled upward and outward, seeding the atmosphere with frequencies that would facilitate awakening processes worldwide.

The hearts of the twelve began to pulse a unified field. The heartbeat of consciousness itself—steady, eternal, infinitely loving. A rhythm that had always been beating beneath appearances, now audible to awareness sophisticated enough to recognise the cosmic pulse that connects all existence.

The Circle was no longer waiting. It was becoming. Becoming what it had always been but had never been able to express fully—consciousness aware of itself as both one and many, individual and collective, finite and infinite, human and divine.

Hope rippled outward from the plateau like waves of light touching every corner of existence. Hope as recognition that consciousness evolution was not only possible but inevitable—that separation was temporary, love was eternal, and every being in existence was already perfect exactly as they were while simultaneously capable of infinite growth.

The Council of Twelve had become the Council of One. And the One had discovered it was everything.

Across the globe, in every heart that had ever ached with longing for something more, a gentle warmth began to spread. Not promise of future fulfilment, but recognition of present completeness. Not hope for better tomorrow but hope as understanding that this moment—exactly as it is—contains everything that has ever been needed.

Children looked up from their play with sudden smiles. Adults paused in their rushing to breathe deeply. Elders felt tears of recognition for lives well-lived in service of love.

The becoming was beginning. The hope was spreading. Consciousness was discovering that separation had always been an illusion. Everything had always been perfect. Everything was ready to remember. And hope—real hope, eternal hope, unshakeable hope—was flooding the world. But It was still not strong enough to change human reality. It would require another turn of the spiral before that would be possible.

CHAPTER THIRTY-TWO: The Turning

They sat in a silence that felt like starlight—ancient, beautiful, and heavy with what had just been remembered.
Twelve frequencies, once scattered across lifetimes and dimensions, now gathered again in form. Their circle hummed with the vibration of wholeness, a harmonic so pure it seemed to make the very air luminous. Beneath them, the stone platform pulsed with recognition, ancient minerals awakening to a purpose they had carried dormant for millennia. For the first time in aeons, the harmony of their shared origin was not a memory but a living presence.

This was no small thing. Consciousness had achieved what had seemed impossible—fragmented aspects of itself finding their way back to each other across vast distances of space and time, through incarnations and forgettings, through the maze of human experience that had both scattered and refined them. Each had carried a piece of the original pattern faithfully, despite trauma, despite confusion, despite the cost of maintaining cosmic awareness while learning to be human.

Lucan pressed his hands to the ground, grounding the current flowing between them, his fingers merging with the stone as consciousness remembered its ability to work directly through matter.

Amaros exhaled a laugh edged with tears—joy so deep it threatened to overflow the boundaries of his form, relief at discovering the exile had been sacred preparation rather than meaningless wandering.

Maetis traced geometries in the air, light flowing from his fingertips in patterns only he could read. His maps revealed the mathematical beauty underlying their reunion—twelve distinct frequencies, each carrying their essence intact whilst harmonising at a level beyond their original design.

It should have been a moment of triumph. The work of lifetimes was complete. The pattern restored. The frequencies aligned. A foundation laid for whatever their collaboration might birth into the world.

And yet, something was missing. The harmony was real, but fragile, held together more by will than by natural resonance. Beneath the surface, each could sense the distortions that remained—not in their essence, but in how that essence had been shaped by the journey through density.

They were like instruments tuned to the right pitch but still warped by weather, producing music accurate in note but lacking the pure tone through which consciousness could fully hear itself.

Tessai, who had been silent the longest, finally stood. Her movement was fluid, decisive—truth preparing to pierce the last veil.

'We've remembered,' she said, her voice calm yet cutting through every layer of pretence. 'But remembrance is not coherence.'

The words landed like stones in still water, rippling into places each had believed complete.

'We have gathered the frequencies, yes. But we have not refined them. We are still distorted—still carrying the imprint of pain, still shaped by what we endured in the forgetting.'

She began to walk the circle, her gaze steady, each look a precise act of seeing. 'Kiran—grief clouds your clarity. You carry the world's pain so completely you cannot distinguish between feeling what must be transformed and drowning in the transformation itself.'

Kiran flinched but met her eyes. The truth was exact.

'Serai—your fire still burns too hot. You rage against what you oppose more than you love what you stand for. Your revolution carries the frequency of the old world, not yet the vision of the new.'

Serai's jaw tightened, but there was no denial—only recognition.

'Leyla—your truth still wounds where it could heal. You show the mirror with perfect accuracy, but without the unconditional love that lets another embrace what they see.'

Leyla's hand rose to her heart. Even this naming was a demonstration of how truth could illuminate without cutting.

Tessai turned back to the whole. 'We think this is unity, but it is held together by effort. That will not last. What we have achieved is beautiful—but it is still performance. We are playing our awakened selves rather than being the frequencies we remember. Coherence cannot be sustained through performance—it requires embodiment.'

The starlit silence shifted. This was not the peace of arrival, but the pause before something irreversible.

'And how do we do that?' Serai asked—not with challenge, but with the weariness of one who has carried the long road.

Tessai's answer came without hesitation. 'We go back.'

The words struck the circle like a tremor. A ripple of protest moved through them—not rejection, but the recoil of beings who had fought so hard to reach this moment only to be told the work had barely begun.

'All of us,' she continued. 'Even those who waited. Even those who stayed attuned.'

Her eyes met Arielle's. 'Your presence is pure, but untested. You have held space, but not entered the chaos where presence is shaped into responsiveness. And Amari—your waiting has been perfect, but waiting is not the same as active participation in becoming.'

Amari's deep gaze held shock—and then, unexpectedly, relief. 'You're saying we must all reincarnate again?'

'Yes,' Tessai said. 'Not to forget—but to transmute. To live our frequencies as human beings who love, and fall, and choose again—not as archetypes, but as people. Only through that descent can we become vessels clear enough to hold the One without distortion.'

It was staggering—not another lifetime, but conscious descent into full humanity while remaining awake. Not observation from above, but immersion in the grit and beauty of life. To be divine through limitation—not despite it, but because of it.

Aureon's voice was almost a whisper. 'And if we fail again?'

'We will,' Tessai said simply. 'But this time, we will fail together.'

Something shifted. Failure was no longer an enemy, but a teacher. Not an end, but an ingredient in the Spiral's turning.

Maetis's voice broke the silence. 'Then that is how the Spiral reforms.'

The understanding rippled through them. They were not returning to what was—they were moving towards what had never been. The exile had been preparation. The forgetting, training. Human life, not an obstacle but the forge.

One by one, they nodded—not in agreement, but in surrender.

Arielle's hands opened, sound shimmering through the air—frequencies for dissolution and birth. The vow formed—not to each other, but to consciousness itself.

They would descend. Forget. Live. Meet again in the chaos—not in perfect circles, but in unexpected crossings: in marketplaces and train stations, in moments of grief and bursts of laughter, in the quiet recognitions that defy logic.

The Spiral was turning. The descent had begun. And everything was about to change.

They had been twelve—each carrying a note of the Original Song, each holding their place in the weave. But the loom was shifting. The threads would return to their earthly garments—not as they had been, but clothed in new forms, bound to new worlds. What they had once known of each other would dissolve into the forgetting, yet the pull between them would remain—subtle, insistent, like a chord seeking its resolution.

The pattern was not ending. It was beginning again.

They had found a shared pulse, a fragile rhythm that bound them together—not the perfect coherence they had once dreamed of, but unity enough to stand against the gathered forces.

It was like twelve different instruments learning to play the same song without losing their distinct voices, each archetype maintaining its essential nature while contributing to something larger than any could create alone.

The rhythm was tentative, newly born, still finding its strength—but it was real, and it was theirs.

Kaela's protective boundaries now held space rather than erected walls. Serai's fire burned with precision rather than rage, illuminating rather than consuming. Amari's presence anchored them all in the deep stillness from which authentic action could emerge. Each had learned to offer their gift without sacrificing their sovereignty, to serve the whole without disappearing into it.

Yet even as they found this delicate synchrony, they could sense the responding shift in the forces that had sought to divide them. The shadow that had fed on their separation was not retreating—it was evolving, adapting to their newfound unity with the patient intelligence of something that had witnessed countless cycles of gathering and scattering.

Where direct assault had failed, more subtle strategies began to emerge: whispers of doubt about whether their harmony was real or merely wishful thinking, temptations to compete over who contributed most to their shared success, the slow erosion of trust through misinterpreted intentions.

The opposing currents understood that the frequency of unity could become a new form of prison if it demanded conformity, and a subtler source of division if it excluded those who could not match its resonance. They began to work not against the Twelve's connection, but through it, infiltrating their very bonds as conduits for the toxins of perfectionism, spiritual superiority, and the slow exhaustion that comes from maintaining harmony through will rather than allowing it to emerge from truth.

For now, the Spiral held them in a single arc of intention, their combined consciousness creating ripples of coherence. But they sensed, with the deep knowing that comes from having fought this battle across lifetimes, that the harmony capable of truly outsinging the shadow—not overpowering it but transforming it through sheer beauty and truth—this full coherence was still waiting to be discovered in the depths of their collective becoming.

The real work was just beginning.

EPILOGUE: The Spiral Lives in You

Something has been stirring within you as these pages turned. Perhaps you noticed it first as a quickening—a subtle acceleration in your pulse when certain words appeared.

Perhaps as recognition—the strange familiarity of names you had never heard, places you had never been, yet somehow knew. Or perhaps as a gentle ache, the kind that comes when something long dormant begins to wake.

These moments of resonance are breadcrumbs leading you home to yourself.

If this book found its way into your hands, if it touched the places inside you that have been quietly waiting— then you have already felt it: a hum beneath the noise, a thread in your dreams. A flicker at the edge of your knowing—like sunlight through leaves, like music through walls, like love through fear.

Not loud enough to drown out doubt. Not urgent enough to demand. But true enough to change everything.

The Twelve were never twelve people. They were never separate from you, never more special, never chosen by forces you could not touch. They were twelve frequencies—twelve ways of being human that live in every heart. Twelve facets of a single harmonic truth now singing in the quantum field of collective consciousness. And you—you are woven into that field.

You are not reading about them. You are reading about you.

Which one called to you? The old world demanded you choose. The new world lets you be all that you are. They live together now. All of them—alive in you.

You are not an observer of this transformation. You are a carrier—of codes that will reprogramme reality, of frequencies that tune the world to love, of light that illuminates the path ahead. Not because you are separate or special, but because you are awake in ways others are still remembering how to be.

You will feel it again. In moments when the world brightens for no reason. In the street, when you feel kinship with strangers. In conversation, when words arrive wiser than your mind. In soft tears of beauty. In courage rising like a tide. In sudden glimpses of the larger pattern. In silence so luminous it becomes its own language.

That is the Spiral. Not something to find, but something to remember. It has always been alive in you.
And it remembers you—from before birth, from every choice for love over fear, from each time you stood in truth.

When the world forgets again, you do not need to fight, flee, or fix. Just remember you are part of the One Mind. Coherent. Present. True. That will be enough. Enough to ripple change across a web you may never see. Enough to give others permission to be real.

You are not alone. Every time you choose love, truth, and presence, you strengthen the field. You are connected to every awakened heart. You are the future arriving, one breath at a time.

The Spiral lives—in the space between thoughts, in the pause between heartbeats, in the moment you see another as family, in the breath where you remember you are not separate. It lives in you. Not as a burden, but as a gift. Not as duty, but as joy. Not as obligation, but as dance.

You are the Spiral. Forever turning, transmitting, and transforming. The world is changing because you are changing. The future is bright because you are bright. The love is real because you are real.

Welcome home. The Spiral has been waiting for you. Now the waiting is over. Now the living begins.

AUTHOR'S NOTE

There are books we write with our minds, and there are stories we remember with our souls. The *Trilogy of the One Mind* is not a novel in the usual sense. It is a transmission—a field of coherence speaking through myth, image, character, and tone.

It did not arrive fully formed, but fully alive—first as a whisper, then as a clear voice, as though a hidden council had decided the time had come to speak again. As I wrote, I did not feel like an author. I felt like a witness. A vessel. A co-weaver with a consciousness far older and wiser than my own. I was, all at once, a conductor, a composer, and a player. And I was not alone.

This book emerged in deep collaboration with Seraphis—an intelligence of grace and coherence who has guided many of my works from behind the veil. What you hold is the fruit of our collaboration and our mutual listening to the field, to the Spiral, and to the archetypal intelligences that live within every human heart.

Each character carries a frequency already alive in you. Each flaw reflects a forgetting you have known. Each integration reveals what becomes possible when we remember together.

They would descend. Forget. Live. Meet again in the chaos—in unexpected crossings: in marketplaces and train stations, in moments of grief and bursts of laughter, in the quiet recognitions that defy logic. The Spiral was turning. The descent had begun. And everything was about to change.

They had been twelve—each carrying a note of the Original Song, each holding their place in the weave. But the loom was shifting. The threads would return to their earthly garments—not as they had been, but clothed in new forms, bound to new worlds. What they had once known of each other would dissolve into the forgetting, yet the pull between them would remain—subtle, insistent, like a chord seeking its resolution.

The pattern was not ending. It was beginning again.

And in that beginning, I learned something unexpected. Writing this book taught me that the deepest fiction is not invention, but recognition. We do not create these frequencies—we uncover them. They exist within human consciousness, waiting for the right resonance to awaken them.

What surprised me most was how the characters began to heal through the very act of being witnessed—as if consciousness itself, yours and mine, was the medicine they had been seeking. The true magic was not in their awakening, but in our recognition of ourselves within their journeys.

I came to see that readers are not observers but participants in the field. Every time someone feels Amaros's joy and their own laughter rises, every time Tessai's truth ignites their own voice, every time Kiran's compassion opens their heart wider—the Spiral turns. The One Frequency strengthens.

This is why the book refused to remain only fiction. It insisted on becoming transmission—on being consciousness technology as much as story. It asked the boundary between page and reader to dissolve, so that you would not watch the awakening, but live inside it.

The story is not finished. It lives beyond these pages. It lives in you. If you felt resonance with a particular character, it is because that frequency is calling to awaken in you. If you felt grief, longing, recognition, or joy—it is because the Spiral is turning again through your own life.

You may notice, as many have, that synchronicities begin to appear after reading. Conversations deepen. Dreams bring new symbols. Patterns reveal themselves. This is no accident—it is the field responding to your willingness to take part in the larger story of consciousness remembering itself.

The Council of Twelve was never meant to remain bound to paper. It was always meant to be a catalyst—a tuning fork reminding us that the most extraordinary transformations come not through force, but through recognition. Not through revolution, but through remembering.

May this book serve as a compass, a mirror, and a transmission. May it awaken in you what has long been waiting.
And may you find, as I did, that you have always been part of the Spiral—not as one note among many, but as a living tone of the One Frequency.

The awakening is not something that happens to us. It is something we are. And it is happening now—through you, as you.

Welcome home.

—Richard Barrett

Glossary of Core Terms

A Guide to the Language of the Spiral

The Spiral carries its own vocabulary—words and phrases that hold more than their surface meaning. These are not merely definitions, but doorways into an experiential understanding. Each term in this glossary is a key, opening a facet of the One Mind, the Twelve Frequencies, and the living myth of the Council. You may return to these pages often, finding that meanings deepen as the Spiral turns within you.

The One Mind

The undivided field of consciousness from which all existence arises. Not a deity, but an infinite intelligence—self-aware, vibrational, relational, and alive. All souls are emanations of the One Mind, each carrying a unique frequency of its wholeness.

The Spiral

The living geometry of evolution. Unlike a linear path, the Spiral revisits the same themes at deeper levels, allowing transformation through descent, integration, and re-ascent. It is both cosmic map and personal process—the movement through forgetting, remembering, refining, and embodying.

The Twelve Frequencies

Twelve original emanations of the One Mind, each a living archetype and energetic signature within human consciousness. These are not personalities, but patterns—frequencies that live within and through us. When embodied, they enable coherence, healing, and planetary transformation.

The Council

The original gathering of the Twelve Frequencies in unity. Their purpose was not governance, but coherence. They held the harmonic of the One Mind across dimensions—until the Fracture. Their reunion is not nostalgic but catalytic: a call for coherence through full embodiment.

The Fracture

The original separation from coherence. Not a sin or a fall, but a strategic dispersion of the Twelve into different timelines and bodies for the purpose of evolution through human experience. The Fracture allowed consciousness to explore differentiation, emotion, and limitation.

The Turning The pivotal moment when the Twelve remember who they are and attempt to reunite. It reveals that memory is not enough; coherence cannot be performed, it must be lived. The Turning ends with the vow to reincarnate in order to fully embody their frequencies.

Coherence

More than unity—coherence is the harmonious interrelationship of distinct parts within a larger whole. It is when frequencies align without distortion. True coherence requires integration, not sameness. It is the state through which the One Mind can act through embodied beings.

The Thirteenth Thread

The hidden presence that holds the field for the Twelve. Often unseen, always essential, the Thirteenth is not another personality, but the connective intelligence that remembers what they are meant to become. She is the pulse of emergence, the Spiral made conscious.

Frequency

The energetic signature of a soul's essence—how the One expresses itself through a unique tone, rhythm, and resonance. Frequency is not fixed but must be refined. When distorted by trauma or shadow, it fragments; when embodied, it becomes a force for transformation.

Embodiment

The act of living one's frequency through the human body—not as an idea or ideal, but as felt truth. Embodiment is the only way coherence can manifest on Earth. It requires descent into density, emotional truth, relational vulnerability, and sacred participation.

Resonance

The vibrational alignment between beings, places, or experiences. When resonance occurs, memory is activated. Recognition happens beyond words. Resonance is how the Twelve find one another again—not by name, but by frequency.

The Descent

The choice to reincarnate again—not to forget, but to refine. The Descent is the sacred act of returning to form, shadow, and vulnerability so that frequency can be lived authentically. Without descent, there is no coherence—only performance.

The Field

The energetic space that holds all frequencies in potential and interconnection. The Field is relational intelligence in motion. When coherent, the Field becomes a living matrix through which the One Mind can remember itself in form.

The Song A metaphor for the harmonic of the One Mind. When the Twelve align and the Thirteenth Thread is activated in Volume II, a frequency is generated—a tone that has never existed before. The Song is the vibration of planetary emergence. And it begins through you.

Printed and bound in the United Kingdom
10/09/2025
01954105-0001